C^{THE}HAMPIONSHIP 1999

FOOTBALL AND HURLING

Follow your dreams
with the Eircell GAA All Stars.

DEDICATED TO

TRISH, JOHN BRIAN & SARAH MARIE

By the same author:
Football Captains 1940 – 1993
The Championship 1995 – Football and Hurling
The Championship 1996 – Football and Hurling
The Championship 1997 – Football and Hurling
The Championship 1998 – Football and Hurling

Above books and *'Championship '99'* are available from
Sliabh Bán Productions Ltd.,
P.O. Box No. 6369,
Dublin 6

HERE'S A MUSEUM WHERE YOU CAN SMASH UP SOME OF THE EXHIBITS.

INTERACTIVE TESTS OF YOUR HURLING AND FOOTBALL SKILLS
ARE JUST A SMALL PART OF THE MAJOR ENTERTAINMENT EXPERIENCE
AWAITING YOU IN THE GAA MUSEUM AT CROKE PARK.

RANGING FROM HISTORICAL EXHIBITS OF TIMES GONE BY
TO THE INFORMATIVE TOUCHSCREEN TECHNOLOGY OF THE MODERN DAY,
THIS MUSEUM GIVES YOU A UNIQUE INSIGHT INTO IRELAND'S
SPORTING, CULTURAL AND SOCIAL TRADITIONS.

MAKE SURE YOU DROP IN.

The
GAA MUSEUM
CROKE PARK

CHAMPIONSHIP 1999

FOOTBALL AND HURLING

The Complete Record

Brian Carthy

Sliabh Bán Productions Limited
P.O. Box No. 6369, Dublin 6.

© Brian Carthy, 1999

ISBN 0 9532236 2 0

A CIP record of this book is available from the British Library.

Cover Design: Mary Guinan, Temple of Design
Photography: Sportsfile
Layout and design: Temple of Design
Printed in Ireland by Kilkenny People Printing

ACKNOWLEDGMENTS

The author and publisher would like to thank all the people who assisted with the publication of this book.

Special thanks also to Paddy Goode, Jim O'Sullivan, Frank Greally, Danny Lynch, Mary Guinan,
Deirdre McGreevy, Eircell, Seán MacAonghusa, Katherine O'Connor and Deirdre O'Connell;
to all our advertisers, and to Sportsfile for permission to use their photographs.

Contents

MESSAGE FROM THE PRESIDENT

I always look forward with great enthusiasm to reading Brian Carthy's Championship book, which covers every detail of the summer's Hurling and Football action. The increased popularity of Gaelic Games in recent years has coincided with the welcome proliferation of GAA publications. These have covered virtually every aspect of the Association and our games. Until recently, however, there has been no comprehensive record of our Championships, recording details that would prove vital for future historians of our games. Brian Carthy, commentator, broadcaster, analyst and aficionado of Gaelic Games, has redressed this omission with his splendid books.

Brian's passion for our games, his knowledge and his attention to detail is evident in his wonderful commentaries, Sunday after Sunday, through the medium of RTÉ Radio. In this record of the Championships, Brian transfers his love of the games and his energies to produce the definitive record of the 1999 Championship, speckled with gems of information and details obvious and relevant only when seen chronicled.

I would like to extend by gratitude and congratulations to Brian for his commitment, energy and initiative in producing another unique record of our Championships. I wish it well and hope that many more publications will emerge from his prolific pen in the new millennium.

Go raibh míle maith agat agus rath Dé ar an obair.

Seosamh Mac Donncha,
Uachtarán
Cumann Lúthchleas Gael

Introduction

IT WAS YET ANOTHER EXCITING AND TENSION-FILLED year in both the Hurling and Football Championships. There were no fewer than thirty-seven games in the Football Championship with twenty games in the Hurling Championship and this book contains reports on all fifty-seven games. Every one will have his or her own special memory of a year in which Meath, under the guidance of long-serving manager, Seán Boylan won the All-Ireland football title and Jimmy Barry-Murphy's young Cork side claimed the hurling crown.

Meath began their Championship campaign on Sunday June 6 with victory over Wicklow at Croke Park by 2-10 to 0-6 in a game where 'Man of the Match' Graham Geraghty scored 1-4.

The first Sunday in July saw Meath back in Croke Park again with Offaly providing the opposition in the Leinster Championship semi-final. Seán Boylan's team produced a marvellous second-half display that Offaly simply could not match on the day. Ollie Murphy scored the crucial goal as Meath advanced to the Leinster Final on a 1-13 to 0-9 scoreline. Meath defeated arch-rivals Dublin in the Leinster Final by 1-14 to 0-12 on an August Sunday when Ollie Murphy was the outstanding player on view and finished the game with a personal tally of 1-5. Meath booked their place in the All-Ireland Final with a deserved 0-15 to 2-5 semi-final victory over an Armagh side that scored just once in the second half. Admittedly, the Ulster Champions were reduced to fourteen players in the 54th minute when full-back Gerard Reid was sent-off for a second bookable offence. Meath faced the Munster Champions Cork in the All-Ireland Final on the last Sunday in September and the men from the Royal County proved their pedigree once again by emerging victorious on a 1-11 to 1-8 scoreline to claim their seventh title.

* * * * * * * * * * * * * * * *

Cork hurlers faced up to neighbours Waterford in the Munster semi-final at Semple Stadium on Sunday June 13 with a team containing no fewer than six players new to Championship hurling. Manager Jimmy Barry-Murphy was criticised in some quarters for selecting such an inexperienced team but the players repaid his faith in them. Inspired by midfielder Mickey O'Connell, who scored eight points, Cork showed commendable character to gain a deserved victory by 0-24 to 1-15. Jimmy Barry-Murphy raced on to the field afterwards to embrace his players in a rare show of emotion from him.

On to the Munster Final on July 4 and a controversial goal from Joe Deane set Cork on the road to victory by 1-15 to 0-14 against mighty Clare at Semple Stadium. Clare forward David Forde missed a close-in free near the finish, which could have levelled scores, but thereafter Cork pulled clear and won by four points to claim their first Munster title in seven years.

Cork and Offaly produced a classic All-Ireland Hurling semi-final in wet conditions at Croke Park on the second Sunday in August. There were emotional scenes at the finish as Cork qualified for the All-Ireland Final for the first time since 1992 with a 0-19 to 0-16 scoreline. Mighty Cork centre-half-back, Brian Corcoran summed it up aptly afterwards when he said: 'It was a brilliant game to win, and terrible to lose.'

And Corcoran once again turned in a superb performance in the All-Ireland Final as Cork defeated favourites Kilkenny by a single point on a 0-13 to 0-12 scoreline. Unfortunately, I was admitted to hospital in early September and missed both the hurling and football finals but I was kept up to date through newspapers, radio and television.

I would like to thank my good friends, Jim O'Sullivan of the Examiner Newspaper and Paddy Goode of RTE for their valued assistance in ensuring that all deadlines were met.

It was another wonderful year in hurling and football and heartiest congratulations to Meath and Cork who proved to be two outstanding All-Ireland Champions!

Brian Carthy

ALL-IRELAND SENIOR FOOTBALL CHAMPIONSHIP FINAL

MEATH versus CORK

CROKE PARK

REFEREE: MICHAEL CURLEY (GALWAY)

RESULT: MEATH 1-11 CORK 1-8

IT WAS A DAY OF UNBRIDLED JOY FOR MEATH footballers and their inspirational manager, Seán Boylan – a man apart – as the Royal County claimed their seventh All-Ireland title and the last of the Millenium, exactly fifty years after Brian Smyth captained the county to win their first crown in 1949. That wonderful ambassador of sport, Seán Boylan, was at the helm for four of those All-Ireland victories in 1987, 1988, 1996 and again this year – a proud record which serves to underline his pedigree as one of the greatest managers in the history of the game. Captain Graham Geraghty was one happy man as he stood on the podium in the centre of Croke Park and addressed the Meath faithful all around the famous ground, before eventually raising the Sam Maguire Cup to the heavens amid deafening noise. It was a famous victory for Meath but one could not but feel sympathy for a gallant Cork side and their manager Larry Tompkins, who has certainly assembled a fine squad of players that will surely continue to challenge for major honours in the years ahead. Cork had high hopes of adding the football title to the hurling crown, won two weeks earlier, but it was not to be, as Meath proved the masters and Seán Óg Ó hAilpín was deprived the honour of joining Teddy McCarthy in the history books. McCarthy still remains the only player to win All-Ireland senior football and hurling medals in the one year. Tommy Dowd, ruled out of the starting fifteen because of injury, made a very brief appearance near the finish to complete a perfect day for Meath people everywhere.

The players had to contend with wet conditions, which naturally enough proved extremely difficult, but there were many highlights to savour in the course of a keenly contested and evenly balanced game that mighty Meath deserved to win. As the game entered the final critical phase, Meath had the players that responded to the challenge with ferocious determination that has become the hallmark of Seán Boylan's teams down through the years. Meath were three points ahead at half-time but Cork were handed a lifeline early in the second half when goalkeeper Kevin O'Dwyer saved a penalty from Trevor Giles and shortly afterwards Joe Kavanagh scored a magnificent goal that really brought the game to life. But Meath, displaying their renowned steely resolve, recovered their composure and played some superb direct football to fashion a well-merited victory. Trevor Giles, although off target from a number of frees, was a major influence and played a big role in Meath's

victory, particularly in the closing quarter. Mark O'Reilly was outstanding at corner back; Enda McManus and Darren Fay were also impressive at various stages; Evan Kelly and Graham Geraghty scored three points each from play while Ollie Murphy took his goal splendidly.

Playing against the breeze, Meath jumped into an early lead with a point each from Evan Kelly and Trevor Giles before Mark O'Sullivan opened the scoring for Cork with a point from play in the 10th minute. Joe Kavanagh and Donal Curtis exchanged points but Meath received a tremendous boost in the 25th minute when Ollie Murphy drove the ball past Kevin O'Dwyer in the Cork goal. Both sides continued to miss opportunities but still there were good scores before half-time, none better than from Evan Kelly who scored two fine points to bring his first half tally to three.

Meath led at half-time by 1-5 to 0-5 and had a glorious chance of increasing that lead shortly after the re-start when awarded a penalty after Graham Geraghty was fouled. Trevor Giles' shot was saved by Kevin O'Dwyer and it lifted Cork's spirit no end. Philip Clifford, who more than played his part in the Cork forward line, then landed a point and when Joe Kavanagh blasted the ball to the net, the Munster Champions had moved ahead for the very first time. It was the one stage of the game that Cork really looked like they could win the title, but it was not to be against a doughty Meath side that never accepts defeat. Cork persisted with short passing and it helped Meath to force their way back into the game. It was obvious that Meath rather than Cork raised their game after Kavanagh's goal and that surely sums up the immense quality of the Leinster Champions when under pressure.

Meath outscored Cork by 0-6 to 0-2 in the closing thirty minutes to deservedly win their seventh title, and move into fourth place in the all-time honours list. The Cork forward line struggled in the second half against a strong-running and tight marking Meath defence that delivered early ball to their midfield and forward line to telling effect. Graham Geraghty scored three points for Meath in the second half while Trevor Giles also scored three points including a superb effort from a '45 which pushed Meath 1-9 to 1-8 ahead with little more than ten minutes left to play. Giles and Geraghty added a point each in the closing minutes to seal a famous victory for Meath and their wonderful manager of eighteen years, Seán Boylan.

SCORERS – MEATH: Trevor Giles 0-4; Evan Kelly 0-3; Graham Geraghty 0-3; Ollie Murphy 1-0; Donal Curtis 0-1
CORK: Philip Clifford 0-5; Joe Kavanagh 1-1; Podsie O'Mahony 0-1; Mark O'Sullivan 0-1

Left: Time for celebration – Trevor Giles, Paddy Reynolds and John McDermott

MEATH

Cormac Sullivan

Mark O'Reilly	Darren Fay	Cormac Murphy
Paddy Reynolds	Enda McManus	Hank Traynor
Nigel Crawford	John McDermott	
Evan Kelly	Trevor Giles	Nigel Nestor
Ollie Murphy	Graham Geraghty (Captain)	Donal Curtis

SUBSTITUTES: Richie Kealy for Nigel Nestor; Barry Callaghan for Hank Traynor;
Tommy Dowd for Evan Kelly

CORK

Kevin O'Dwyer

Ronan McCarthy	Seán Óg Ó hAilpín	Anthony Lynch
Ciarán O'Sullivan	Owen Sexton	Martin Cronin
Nicholas Murphy	Micheál O'Sullivan	
Micheál Cronin	Joe Kavanagh	Podsie O'Mahony
Philip Clifford (Captain)	Don Davis	Mark O'Sullivan

SUBSTITUTES: Fionán Murray for Micheál O'Sullivan; Fachtna Collins for Micheál Cronin;
Michael O'Donovan for Podsie O'Mahony

MEATH
BACK ROW L TO R: Trevor Giles, John McDermott, Graham Geraghty, Darren Fay, Cormac Sullivan, Nigel Crawford, Hank Traynor, Nigel Nestor and Cormac Murphy.
FRONT ROW L TO R: Mark O'Reilly, Donal Curtis, Evan Kelly Paddy Reynolds, Ollie Murphy, Enda McManus.

CORK
BACK ROW L TO R: Mark O'Sullivan, Joe Kavanagh, Nicholas Murphy, Micheál O'Sullivan, Ronan McCarthy, Micheál Cronin, Seán Óg Ó hAilpín.
FRONT ROW L TO R: Owen Sexton, Podsie O'Mahony, Ciarán O'Sullivan, Philip Clifford, Kevin O'Dwyer, Anthony Lynch, Martin Cronin, Don Davis.

SUNDAY, MAY 9, 1999

LEINSTER SENIOR FOOTBALL CHAMPIONSHIP (PRELIMINARY ROUND)

WESTMEATH versus CARLOW

DR. CULLEN PARK (CARLOW)

REFEREE: NIALL BARRETT (CORK)

RESULT: WESTMEATH 2-10 CARLOW 1-8

SENSATIONAL! Cork referee Niall Barrett was the centre of controversy on a wet and dreary day at Dr. Cullen Park after he sent off no fewer than six players and handed out fourteen yellow cards. This was a quite extraordinary game by any standards and the first time ever in the history of the Senior Football Championship that a referee felt it necessary to send off six players. I was commentating on the game for RTE Radio Sport and was as surprised as anyone else at the manner in which the referee handed out so many cards, some for what appeared to be no more than trivial offences. Because it was the first day that the disciplinary rules approved by Congress were being applied, I checked with Niall Barrett before the game to establish how he was going to apply the rules. He made it abundantly clear that a yellow card would be shown for the first indiscretion and that would be followed by a yellow and red card for another offence. Clearly the referee mistakenly applied the wrong rules which he maintained was by instruction from a higher authority. Pandemonium ensued. Gardai escorted Barrett off the pitch at the end of the match.

Carlow defenders Johnny Kavanagh and Ken Walker along with Westmeath midfielder Rory O'Connell were each dismissed after receiving a second yellow card. A few days earlier, O'Connell had been given a one-month suspension for his involvement in a tunnel incident at half-time during the Westmeath/Wicklow League game at Cusack Park in February. The Athlone clubman was cleared to line out against Carlow, as he had played no game in the previous month.

Carlow corner-back Brian Farrell and Westmeath corner-forward Kenny Lyons were red-carded for their involvement in a fracas late in the first half while Carlow centre-half-forward Seán Kavanagh was given his marching orders for a foul on Damien Healy in the second-half of what was a bizarre game. Barrett was appointed to referee the game by the new Central Referees Appointments Committee, who have responsibility for the appointments of referees for all games under the jurisdiction of the Central Council and for Provincial Senior Championship games.

There was drama even before the start. Westmeath decided to withdraw their four under 21 players from the team because of their involvement in the All-Ireland Under 21 Final against Kerry the following weekend. Fergal Murray, Aidan Canning, David O'Shaughnessy and Des Dolan were replaced in the starting fifteen by David Murphy, Aidan Lyons, John Cooney and Kenny Lyons. Dolan made an appearance late in the game replacing Kieran Ryan.

Carlow got off to a wonder start after little more than a minute when a sideline ball from midfielder Garvan Ware slipped through the hands of Westmeath goalkeeper Aidan Lennon and into the net for the first goal of the new Championship season. But almost immediately, Westmeath were back on level terms when full-forward Martin Flanagan steered the ball past Carlow goalkeeper John Brennan. The game was on in earnest. Ger Heavin edged Westmeath ahead before Carlow full-forward Johnny Nevin replied with a point to level the match for the second time. Six minutes had elapsed when Carlow full back Andrew Corden became the first player to receive a yellow card in 'Championship '99. By the 15th minute, Johnny Kavanagh, Johnny Nevin, Rory O'Connell and Joe Murphy had all being shown yellow cards. Shortly before the midway stage of the first half, championship debutante, Johnny Kavanagh from the Leighlinbridge club received his marching orders, the first player to be dismissed in 'Championship '99.

Soon the football began to take a back seat as the referee became the focus of attention as he continued to brandish yellow cards and lay down the law. Ken Walker, Russell Casey, Dermot Brady and John Cooney were added to the list of yellow card recipients. Despite the obvious distractions, both sides spared nothing in endeavour in what were deplorable conditions. Players found it difficult to cope with the greasy surface and the heavy rain, which fell incessantly throughout.

Ger Heavin scored three further points to push Westmeath 1-4 to 1-1 ahead by the 19th minute. Carlow corner-forward Mark Dowling converted two frees to reduce the margin to the minimum before the in-form Heavin landed his fifth point with a superb effort from play in the 25th minute.

There was be no further score for the remainder of the half, although Heavin had a penalty saved by Carlow goalkeeper John Brennan following a foul on Paul Conway. Earlier, Brennan came off his line to deprive John Cooney a certain goal. Carlow corner-back, Brian Farrell and Westmeath corner-forward, Kenny Lyons were both sent-off for their involvement in a fracas in injury-time.

Westmeath led at the interval by 1-5 to 1-3 but two points from play by the impressive Jody Morrissey, a grandson of the 'Boy Wonder', Tommy Murphy, brought the sides level within two minutes of the re-start. Mark Dowling tacked on a point from a free to leave Carlow in front for only the second time in the game.

C(ntre-half-back, Ken Walker was shown the yellow card followed by the red in the 41st minute, as Carlow were reduced to twelve players. The referee also flashed the yellow card at Pa Kavanagh and Garvan Ware before Seán Kavanagh was sent to the line. While the game of cards continued to be played, Ger Heavin and Mark Staunton kicked a point each for Westmeath while Jody Morrissey and Noel Doyle replied with points for Carlow. Rory O'Connell was the sixth player to be dismissed in the 53rd minute to leave just twenty-four players remaining on the field.

Ger Heavin levelled the game for the sixth time with a superb point from play and, from there on, Westmeath's numerical advantage proved crucial as eleven-man Carlow fought valiantly to keep the game alive. Heavin sent over a free for the lead point. There was despair for brave Carlow when Jody Morrissey's flicked effort flashed narrowly wide. The highly impressive Morrissey was also unlucky near the finish when his shot for the equalising point just failed to find the target.

The game was well and truly decided when Martin Flanagan crashed the ball to the net for his second goal that left Westmeath four points clear. Fittingly, 'Man of the Match' Heavin had the final say with a point from a free, his ninth of the game. It was just as well that Heavin was on form for Westmeath, for apart from two-goal hero, Martin Flanagan, only one other player, substitute Mark Staunton found the target for the midlanders.

Carlow later objected to the result. The Games Administration Committee of the G.A.A. considered the referee's report in relation to disciplinary matters only, while the Leinster Council dealt with Carlow's contention that the result of the game was not valid on the grounds that the referee misapplied the rules.

The GAC ruled that Carlow's Johnny Kavanagh and Ken Walker along with Rory O'Connell of Westmeath were incorrectly sent-off. Kenny Lyons was handed a one-month ban while Carlow's Seán Kavanagh and Brian Farrell both requested oral hearings. Carlow's case was strengthened by the GAC's decision and the Leinster delegates came out strongly in favour of a refixture. Westmeath appealed to the Management Committee and Carlow's hopes of a reprieve disappeared when the high-powered Committee overturned the Leinster Council's decision to refix the game.

After much drama and controversy, Carlow thus became the first team to be knocked out of Championship '99!

SCORERS – WESTMEATH: Ger Heavin 0-9; Martin Flanagan 2-0; Mark Staunton 0-1
CARLOW: Jody Morrissey 0-3; Mark Dowling 0-3; Garvan Ware 1-0; Noel Doyle 0-1;
Johnny Nevin 0-1

WESTMEATH

Aidan Lennon

Dermot Brady	David Murphy	Russell Casey
Aidan Lyons	David Mitchell	Kieran Ryan

Rory O'Connell (Captain)   John Cooney

Damien Healy	Paul Conway	Shane Colleary
Ger Heavin	Martin Flanagan	Kenny Lyons

SUBSTITUTES: Mark Staunton for Shane Colleary; Eddie Casey for Damien Healy;
Des Dolan for Kieran Ryan

CARLOW

John Brennan

Brian Farrell	Andrew Corden	Paud O'Dwyer
Joe Murphy (Captain)	Ken Walker	Johnny Kavanagh

Garvan Ware   Jody Morrissey

Noel Doyle	Seán Kavanagh	Willie Quinlan
Mark Dowling	Johnny Nevin	Pa Kavanagh

SUBSTITUTES: Joe Byrne for Paud O'Dwyer; Peter Kingston for Mark Dowling;
Mark Carpenter for Pa Kavanagh

WESTMEATH
BACK ROW L TO R: Aidan Lyons, Martin Flanagan, Russell Casey, Aidan Lennon, Rory O'Connell, Paul Conway, Damien Healy, David Murphy
FRONT ROW L TO R: David Mitchell, Ger Heavin, Kieran Ryan, Dermot Brady, Shane Colleary, Kenny Lyons, John Cooney

CARLOW
BACK ROW L TO R: Paud O'Dwyer, Garvan Ware, Andrew Corden, Ken Walker, Jody Morrissey, Seán Kavanagh, Noel Doyle, Mark Dowling
FRONT ROW L TO R: John Brennan, Johnny Nevin, Willie Quinlan, Joe Murphy, Pa Kavanagh, Johnny Kavanagh, Brian Farrell

SUNDAY, MAY 9, 1999

LEINSTER SENIOR FOOTBALL CHAMPIONSHIP PRELIMINARY ROUND

LONGFORD versus WEXFORD

KENNEDY PARK (NEW ROSS)

REFEREE: NOEL COONEY (OFFALY)

RESULT: LONGFORD 1-13 WEXFORD 0-16 (A DRAW)

CENTRE-HALF-BACK RORY STAFFORD scored the equalising point in injury-time to earn Wexford a replay in what was an absorbing game at Kennedy Park in New Ross. Stafford's well-taken point from play after a quick free from Leigh O'Brien was one of the many highlights of a highly competitive and keenly contested clash between two well-matched teams.

Both sets of players deserve every credit for producing such high quality fare in winter-like conditions that would be more seasonable in December than the second Sunday in May. I watched a video of the game on the Monday and found it to be most entertaining with some wonderful passages of play and equally impressive scores from both sides.

Wexford never once held the lead and their hopes of salvaging the game looked remote when impressive Longford midfielder Enda Barden pushed his side two points ahead, 1-13 to 0-14, with less than one minute remaining. But Wexford displayed tremendous character to claw their way back into the game in the dying moments. Firstly, Scott Doran kicked a point from play and then Rory Stafford levelled the game with a superb point. It was a tremendous comeback by Wexford and atoned somewhat for their disappointing showing in last year's Leinster Championship replay, which Longford won by 0-16 to 2-7 in Pearse Park.

Longford midfielder David Hannify opened the scoring with a point from play but that was cancelled out by a fine effort from Wexford captain Jim Byrne. Padraic Davis edged Longford ahead before championship debutante, Paul Barden, a player of real quality, then scored the only goal of the game after just seven minutes play to put Longford 1-2 to 0-1 ahead and in the driving seat.

As the game settled to a pattern, it became clear that Longford corner forward Padraic Davis and his Wexford counterpart Scott Doran were both eager and ready for the task at hand. Both players swapped points before Wexford half-forward John Hegarty converted a free. Young Martin Mulleady, in his first championship game, was superb at corner back for Longford against no less a player that Jason Lawlor while midfielder Enda Barden produced a tour-de-force display. Rory Stafford and Leigh O'Brien were strong and forceful in the Wexford defence and thwarted Longford on many occasions.

Favoured by the strong wind, Longford had built up a five points lead by the 32nd minute, thanks mainly to the accuracy of Padraic Davis, who scored four points in the first half. Terry Drake and Niall Sheridan, after Colin Hannify's shot came off the post, also found the range with a point each from play for Longford. Scott Doran's third point left Wexford 1-7 to 0-6 in arrears at half-time. John Hegarty could have closed the gap further but untypically he shot wide from a close-in free.

Longford's four point half-time lead looked vulnerable, given the strength of the breeze facing them in the second- half, and their supporters had good reason to fret when Scott Doran and Leigh O'Brien scored a point each within six minutes of the re-start. O'Brien's point was a real blockbuster! Paul Barden answered Longford's call and his powerful goal-bound shot was brilliantly tipped over the crossbar by Wexford goalkeeper, Ollie Murphy. Still, Wexford's revival continued apace and three points from play in quick succession, including two from Michael Mahon and one from John Hegarty, brought the sides level for the second time. Longford responded in style and outscored Wexford by 0-3 to 0-1 over the next ten minutes, during which Enda Barden, Padraic Davis and Paul Barden landed a point each. Paul Barden's score was nothing short of inspirational. He chipped the ball into his hand at full speed and racing forward flat-out, drove the ball between the posts. It was a wonderful point, which left Longford 1-12 to 0-13 ahead with six minutes remaining. Leigh O'Brien and Enda Barden exchanged points to keep the pot boiling until Scott Doran and Rory Stafford sent over the match-saving points. An excellent game!

SCORERS – LONGFORD: Padraic Davis 0-6; Paul Barden 1-2; Enda Barden 0-2;
David Hannify 0-1; Niall Sheridan 0-1; Terry Drake 0-1
WEXFORD: Scott Doran 0-5; John Hegarty 0-3; Leigh O'Brien 0-3; Michael Mahon 0-2;
Jim Darcy 0-1; Jim Byrne 0-1; Rory Stafford 0-1

LONGFORD

John Joe Reilly

| Martin Mulleady | Donal Ledwith | Robert Forbes |
| Ciaran Keogh | Frank McNamee | Trevor Smullen |

David Hannify   Enda Barden

| Paul Barden | Colin Hannify (Captain) | Derek Farrell |
| Terry Drake | Niall Sheridan | Padraic Davis |

SUBSTITUTES: Enda Ledwith for Robert Forbes; Dessie Barry for Ciaran Keogh

WEXFORD

Ollie Murphy

| Darragh Breen | Mick Kavanagh | Donal Redmond |
| Colin Sunderland | Rory Stafford | Leigh O'Brien |

John Harrington   Jim Darcy

| John Hegarty | Pat Forde | Jim Byrne (Captain) |
| Scott Doran | Michael Mahon | Jason Lawlor |

SUBSTITUTES: Mattie Forde for Jason Lawlor; Ollie Kinlough for Jim Byrne

LONGFORD
BACK ROW L TO R: Frank McNamee, David Hannify, Niall Sheridan, Enda Barden, John Joe Reilly, Terry Drake, Paul Barden, Ciaran Keogh
FRONT ROW L TO R: Robbie Forbes, Padraic Davis, Colin Hannify, Martin Mulleady, Derek Farrell, Donal Ledwith, Trevor Smullen

WEXFORD
BACK ROW L TO R: Darragh Breen, Donal Redmond, Jim Byrne, John Harrington, Pat Forde, Mick Kavanagh, Rory Stafford, Michael Mahon
FRONT ROW L TO R: Scott Doran, Jim Darcy, Ollie Murphy, Leigh O'Brien, Jason Lawlor, John Hegarty, Colin Sunderland

SUNDAY, MAY 16, 1999

LEINSTER SENIOR FOOTBALL CHAMPIONSHIP PRELIMINARY ROUND (REPLAY)

LONGFORD versus WEXFORD

PEARSE PARK (LONGFORD)

REFEREE: NOEL COONEY (OFFALY)

RESULT: LONGFORD 2-15 WEXFORD 0-11

THERE WAS DELIGHT AMONG PLAYERS and supporters alike at Pearse Park in the aftermath of Longford's most polished and confident performance in the Championship for many a year! And why not! After all, generations of Longford footballers have endured far more lows than highs in their many sojourns in the Leinster Championship. I was covering the game for RTE Radio Sport and was highly-impressed with the quality of football played by this young and eager Longford team, that had many heroes on the day, none more so than wing-back Trevor Smullen. The strong-running Ballymahon player was outstanding all through and scored 1-4 in a 'Man of the Match' performance.

Shell-shocked Wexford, who came from behind to snatch a draw the previous week at New Ross, suffered a major blow after less than four minutes play when full-back Mick Kavanagh was dismissed for a second bookable offence. Kavanagh's sending off altered the course of the game and entirely disrupted Wexford's game plan. Centre-half-back Frank McNamee took up the role as extra man to telling effect as Longford took full advantage of Wexford's misfortune. Pat Forde was switched from centre-half forward to plug the gap in the Wexford full-back line, but it proved a difficult assignment.

Wing-forward Paul Barden belied his tender years with a superb display for Longford and, like Smullen, accounted for 1-4 of his side's total. Barden continually wrong-footed an under pressure Wexford defence, missing the influence of Kavanagh.

Scott Doran had Wexford in front within 20 seconds but the game changed dramatically once Kavanagh was shown the red card. Wexford scored just twice for the remainder of the half – a point each from Leigh O'Brien and John Hegarty – while Longford, favoured by the breeze, took control through a combination of neat passing, solid defence, workmanlike midfield and the accuracy of Paul Barden, Padraic Davis and the speedy Trevor Smullen. Barden's goal in the 33rd minute left Longford 1-8 to 0-3 ahead and further points from Terry Drake and basketball star Smullen ensured the home side had a comfortable ten points lead at the interval.

A point each from John Hegarty and Jason Lawlor early in the second half hinted at a Wexford revival, but their hopes were dashed in the 40th minute when Trevor Smullen finished the ball to the net after a cross from Niall Sheridan.

Wexford fought bravely in the second half thanks mainly to hard-working midfielder, John Harrington, who ran himself to a standstill in an effort to stem the tide. Jason Lawlor, John Hegarty, Leigh O'Brien and Scott Doran all fired over points to give us an insight into Wexford's capabilities and served to demonstrate what might have been possible had Kavanagh not received his marching orders so early in the game. This was a refreshing performance by Longford and great credit is due to manager Michael McCormack for assembling such a well-prepared and highly motivated team.

SCORERS – LONGFORD: Trevor Smullen 1-4; Paul Barden 1-4; Padraic Davis 0-3; Enda Barden 0-2; Terry Drake 0-1; Shane Carroll 0-1
WEXFORD: John Hegarty 0-4; Leigh O'Brien 0-3; Scott Doran 0-2; Jason Lawlor 0-2

LONGFORD

John Joe Reilly

Martin Mulleady   Donal Ledwith   Colin Hannify (Captain)

Enda Ledwith   Frank McNamee   Trevor Smullen

David Hannify   Enda Barden

Derek Farrell   Shane Carroll   Paul Barden

Terry Drake   Niall Sheridan   Padraic Davis

SUBSTITUTES: Robert Forbes for David Hannify; Michael Mulleady for Padraic Davis; Gareth Johnston for Niall Sheridan

---

WEXFORD

Ollie Murphy (Captain)

Seán O'Shaughnessy   Mick Kavanagh   Donal Redmond

Colin Sunderland   Rory Stafford   Leigh O'Brien

John Harrington   Willie Carley

John Hegarty   Pat Forde   Ollie Kinlough

Scott Doran   Michael Mahon   Jason Lawlor

SUBSTITUTES: Mattie Forde for Ollie Kinlough; Darragh Breen for Donal Redmond; Jim Byrne for Mattie Forde

LONGFORD
BACK ROW L TO R: Frank McNamee, David Hannify, Donal Ledwith, Enda Barden, John Joe Reilly, Niall Sheridan, Terry Drake
FRONT ROW L TO R: Derek Farrell, Shane Carroll, Paul Barden, Colin Hannify, Martin Mulleady, Padraic Davis, Trevor Smullen, Enda Ledwith

WEXFORD
BACK ROW L TO R: Michael Mahon, Willie Carley, Pat Forde, Seán O'Shaughnessy, Ollie Kinlough, John Harrington, Mick Kavanagh, Rory Stafford
FRONT ROW L TO R: Donal Redmond, Scott Doran, Colin Sunderland, Ollie Murphy, Leigh O'Brien, Jason Lawlor, John Hegarty

SUNDAY, MAY 30, 1999

LEINSTER SENIOR FOOTBALL CHAMPIONSHIP

WESTMEATH versus LONGFORD

CUSACK PARK (MULLINGAR)

REFEREE: BRIAN WHITE (WEXFORD)

RESULT: WESTMEATH 3-17 LONGFORD 2-9

WESTMEATH PRODUCED A SUPERB display that Longford simply could not match in what was a one-sided encounter at Cusack Park. Much was expected of Longford after their encouraging ten-point replay victory over Wexford at Pearse Park two weeks earlier, but Westmeath, boosted by their All-Ireland Under 21 victory over Kerry, were much the stronger team and at one stage in the second-half led by a staggering nineteen points. Longford, to their credit, continued to battle against the odds and in fact outscored Westmeath by 2-4 to 0-2 in the closing quarter with the goals coming from Niall Sheridan and Trevor Smullen. That scoring spree helped put a level of respectability on the score-board, but was of little consolation to the losers. Westmeath had clearly eased up when nineteen points ahead and Longford took advantage to close the gap at the finish to a more acceptable eleven-point margin. But it is important to urge caution when assessing Westmeath's display as Longford were well below par on the day. Rest assured, Laois will provide a much sterner test for what is still a relatively inexperienced Westmeath side with a defence that has still to be tested.

There were many positive aspects about Westmeath's play and manager Brendan Lowry deserves tremendous credit for the manner in which he has assembled such a high quality team. Westmeath play a delightful brand of open attractive football and have forwards with the ability to take scores. Under 21 star Des Dolan scored 1-6 while Ger Heavin notched 1-5 in what was yet another top-drawer display by the Moate All Whites player.

Heavin, Dolan and Martin Flanagan, who was replaced by Eddie Casey some ten minutes from time, wreaked havoc in the Longford defence and between them finished the game with a total of 3-11. Therein lies the key to Westmeath's victory. By contrast the Longford full-forward line accounted for a mere 1-1 as Terry Drake, Niall Sheridan and Padraic Davis were never allowed any latitude by a tigerish and close-marking Westmeath defence, who recovered well from the loss of full-back Russell Casey through injury as early as the 12th minute. John O'Brien replaced Casey. Fergal Murray was simply outstanding in the Westmeath back line. Longford played quite well in the early stages and only trailed by a single point after sixteen minutes play. The football was of good standard with both sides endeavouring to gain superiority. Longford midfielders David Hannify and Enda Barden were more than holding their own against Rory O'Connell and David O'Shaughnessy but that was soon to change. The floodgates opened when Des Dolan scored Westmeath's first goal midway through the first half. From there on it was one way traffic for the Midlanders.

Martin Flanagan finished the ball to the Longford net in the 27th minute while Ger Heavin put the game beyond the reach of Longford with a fine goal approaching the half-time break. Dominant Westmeath led at the interval by ten points, 3-6 to 0-5, and it was plain for all to see that Longford had not even a remote chance of making a winning comeback.

Westmeath tore out of the traps in the second half and hit over nine unanswered points, including three from Des Dolan, to completely demoralise Longford. Westmeath had built up a nineteen-point advantage, 3-15 to 0-5 entering the final quarter by playing some exhibition football.

Longford had a strong final quarter with goals from Niall Sheridan and Trevor Smullen but at that stage Westmeath had secured victory and a Leinster quarter-final meeting with Laois at Croke Park.

SCORERS – WESTMEATH: Des Dolan 1-6; Ger Heavin 1-5; Martin Flanagan 1-0; Rory O'Connell 0-2; David O'Shaughnessy 0-1; Aidan Canning 0-1; Paul Conway 0-1; Shane Colleary 0-1
LONGFORD: Enda Barden 0-4; Niall Sheridan 1-0; Trevor Smullen 1-0; Paul Barden 0-2; Padraic Davis 0-1; Enda Ledwith 0-1; David Hannify 0-1

WESTMEATH

Dermot Ryan

| Dermot Brady | Russell Casey | Fergal Murray |
| Aidan Lyons | Aidan Canning | Kieran Ryan |

Rory O'Connell (Captain)   David O'Shaughnessy

| Damien Healy | Paul Conway | Shane Colleary |
| Ger Heavin | Martin Flanagan | Des Dolan |

SUBSTITUTES: John O'Brien for Russell Casey; Mark Staunton for Paul Conway; Eddie Casey for Martin Flanagan

---

LONGFORD

John Joe Reilly

| Martin Mulleady | Donal Ledwith | Colin Hannify (Captain) |
| Enda Ledwith | Frank McNamee | Trevor Smullen |

David Hannify   Enda Barden

| Derek Farrell | Shane Carroll | Paul Barden |
| Terry Drake | Niall Sheridan | Padraic Davis |

SUBSITUTES: John Fitzpatrick for Derek Farrell; Robert Forbes for Terry Drake

WESTMEATH
BACK ROW L TO R: Aidan Lyons, Martin Flanagan, Paul Conway, Rory O'Connell, Russell Casey, David O'Shaughnessy, Aidan Canning, Damien Healy
FRONT ROW L TO R: Ger Heavin, Des Dolan, Kieran Ryan, Dermot Brady, Fergal Murray, Shane Colleary, Dermot Ryan

LONGFORD
BACK ROW L TO R: : Frank McNamee, David Hannify, Donal Ledwith, Niall Sheridan, John Joe Reilly, Enda Barden, Paul Barden, Terry Drake, Trevor Smullen
FRONT ROW L TO R: Shane Carroll, Colin Hannify, Martin Mulleady, Padraic Davis, Derek Farrell, Enda Ledwith

SUNDAY, JUNE 6, 1999

LEINSTER SENIOR FOOTBALL CHAMPIONSHIP QUARTER-FINAL

MEATH versus WICKLOW

CROKE PARK

REFEREE: PADDY RUSSELL (TIPPERARY)

RESULT: MEATH 2-10 WICKLOW 0-6

MEATH CRUISED TO VICTORY ON what was yet another 'big day' setback for Wicklow footballers in this the tenth meeting between the counties in the Championship. Wicklow have only beaten Meath once in senior Championship football since 1947 and it was obvious from early in this game that a second victory for the 'Garden County' was an unlikely scenario. Meath suffered a setback before the start when it emerged that towering midfielder John McDermott would be unable to take his place because of flu. Jimmy McGuinness, who partnered championship debutante Nigel Crawford, against the formidable Darren Coffey and Fergus Daly, took McDermott's place.

Meath were forced to play the entire second-half with fourteen players after centre-half-back Hank Traynor was dismissed for a second bookable offence in the 33rd minute, following a foul on Kevin O'Brien. The loss of the Simonstown Gaels player only served to strengthen Meath's resolve and their ten points victory clearly demonstrated the gulf in class between the teams. Enda McManus, who replaced Jimmy McGuinness at half-time, played a very effective role in defence, as Meath manager Seán Boylan reshuffled his team. Wicklow vigorously competed for every ball in the early exchanges and led twice in the opening nine minutes through points from Darren and Ronan Coffey. But once Graham Geraghty equalised with his second point, Meath knuckled down to the business at hand with a determination and style that Wicklow just could not counter. Geraghty had an outstanding game and he proved an unqualified success in his new full-forward position. Wicklow full-back Hugh Kenny had great difficulty coping with the sheer pace of the Meath captain, who scored 1-4 from play. Trevor Giles and Tommy Dowd were both as industrious as ever in what was a sharp and incisive forward division.

1996 'Footballer of the Year', Giles, who suffered a cruciate ligament injury in last year's Leinster Final defeat by Kildare, was in sparkling form and he edged Meath 0-3 to 0-2 ahead with a point from play in the 16th minute. Ollie Murphy, who had earlier blazed a goalbound shot just narrowly wide of the posts, increased Meath's lead with a finely taken point before Barry O'Donovan and Trevor Doyle replied with a point each for Wicklow. Then, Giles struck over two superb points for Meath and as the Wicklow defence came under increasing pressure, Tommy Dowd flicked the ball to the net after a good run by Paddy Reynolds.

Before the first half had run its course, Hank Traynor was shown the red card but it hardly mattered a whit such was Meath's overall strength. Despite playing against the breeze, Meath led by 1-5 to 0-4 at the interval but manager Seán Boylan somehow got his players to lift their game still further after the break. At times, Meath looked awesome and played some exhibition football as Wicklow struggled to stay in touch. Former All-Star Kevin O'Brien, surely one of the finest forwards of his generation, along with Ronan Coffey troubled the Meath defence on occasions, but overall Wicklow lacked the scoring power and guile to make any significant impact.

Giant midfielder Fergus Daly kicked over the opening point of the second half, but it failed to ignite the faltering Wicklow challenge. Indeed, Wicklow only scored once more during the remainder of the game, a point from play by Damien McMahon in the 45th minute while Meath added 1-5 with the goal coming from 'Man of the Match' Graham Geraghty, who once got a trial with Arsenal. Tommy Dowd scored the last two points of the match to illustrate his own willingness for the task at hand, as Meath powered their way to a ten points victory against a below-par Wicklow side. Interestingly, only five Meath players scored while Wicklow had six players on the mark!

SCORERS – MEATH: Graham Geraghty 1-4; Tommy Dowd 1-2; Trevor Giles 0-2; Ollie Murphy 0-1; Ray Magee 0-1
WICKLOW: Darren Coffey 0-1; Ronan Coffey 0-1; Barry O'Donovan 0-1; Trevor Doyle 0-1; Fergus Daly 0-1; Damien McMahon 0-1

MEATH

Cormac Sullivan

Mark O'Reilly   Darren Fay   Cormac Murphy

Paddy Reynolds   Hank Traynor   Donal Curtis

Nigel Crawford   Jimmy McGuinness

Ray Magee   Trevor Giles   Evan Kelly

Tommy Dowd   Graham Geraghty (Captain)   Ollie Muprhy

SUBSTITUTES: Enda McManus for Jimmy McGuinness; Paul Shankey for Paddy Reynolds; Richie Kealy for Donal Curtis

WICKLOW

Tommy Murphy

Mark Coffey   Hugh Kenny   Thomas Burke

Brian Whelan   Barry O'Donovan   Adrian Foley

Darren Coffey (Captain)   Fergus Daly

Damien McMahon   Kevin O'Brien   Ciarán Shannon

Conan Daye   Ronan Coffey   Trevor Doyle

SUBSTITUTES: Brendan Ó hAnnaidh for Ciarán Shannon; Mick Murtagh for Damien McMahon

MEATH
BACK ROW L TO R: Trevor Giles, Graham Geraghty, Jimmy McGuinness, Cormac Murphy, Darren Fay, Cormac Sullivan, Nigel Crawford, Hank Traynor
FRONT ROW L TO R: Mark O'Reilly, Evan Kelly, Donal Curtis, Paddy Reynolds, Ray Magee, Tommy Dowd, Ollie Murphy

WICKLOW
BACK ROW L TO R: Barry O'Donovan, Ronan Coffey, Tommy Murphy, Ciaran Shannon, Darren Coffey, Fergus Daly, Hugh Kenny
FRONT ROW L TO R: Thomas Burke, Brian Whelan, Trevor Doyle, Adrian Foley, Mark Coffey, Damien McMahon, Conan Daye, Kevin O'Brien

SUNDAY, JUNE 6, 1999

LEINSTER SENIOR FOOTBALL CHAMPIONSHIP QUARTER-FINAL

DUBLIN versus LOUTH

CROKE PARK

REFEREE: JOHN BANNON (LONGFORD)

RESULT: DUBLIN 2-15 LOUTH 0-14

THERE WAS TALK BEFORE THIS GAME that Louth had perhaps assembled a team capable of causing an upset against a Dublin side that appeared to be some way short of the finished article. But what transpired was completely at odds with pre-match expectations. The Dubs performed admirably and, despite hitting no fewer than eighteen wides, never looked in any danger of falling at the first hurdle against a Louth team that produced a sub-standard display.

Louth, searching for their first Championship win over the Dubs since 1973, failed to function with any consistent degree of cohesiveness much to the dismay of their loyal supporters who must be wondering if their footballers will ever again make the breakthrough in Leinster.

Ian Robertson, more accustomed to playing in defence, was a huge success at full-forward, and his goal after less than eleven minutes play turned the game firmly in favour of the Dubs. Louth started impressively with a pointed free from Aaron Hoey, but Robertson's goal took the wind out of their sails. Midfielder Seamus O'Hanlon along with Alan Doherty and substitute Colin Kelly, who replaced Seán O'Neill in the 22nd minute, more than kept the Dublin defence on their toes in the opening half. But once Mick O'Keeffe scored Dublin's second goal shortly after the interval there was a sense of inevitability about the outcome. Dublin grew in confidence as Louth visibly wilted, when it became abundantly clear that their Championship ambitions were over for at least another year.

Ciaran Whelan produced a highly impressive display for the Dubs at midfield and his four points from play was no more than he deserved for his all-round skill and awesome work-rate. Declan Darcy was another player to impress and he finished the game as Dublin's top scorer with five points.

Darcy, Brendan O'Brien and Brian Stynes all fired over points to leave Dublin 1-4 to 0-2 ahead by the 19th minute as Louth struggled to keep in touch. Colin Kelly's introduction certainly helped stem the tide and gave Louth much needed strength in attack. The Newtown Blues player won a lot of possession and caused more than a little difficulty for the Dubs back line. Louth enjoyed their best spell following Kelly's introduction and had closed the gap to just three points at the interval.

Declan Darcy and Alan Doherty exchanged points early in the second half but Mick

O'Keeffe's well-taken goal in the 40th minute pushed Dublin six points clear. The margin soon increased to nine courtesy of two points from Darcy and one from Ciaran Whelan to further demoralise the Louth men.

Although Colin Kelly and Martin Farrelly replied with a point each, there was never any possibility of a significant comeback for Louth, who mixed the good with the downright awful throughout the course of the second half. Paddy Christie, Ciaran Whelan, and Brian Stynes scored a point apiece between the 56th and the 64th minute to push Dublin into an unassailable 2-15 to 0-12 lead.

But by that stage the sparkle and competitive edge had long disappeared from the match which once again proved a huge disappointment for Louth players and supporters alike. In the closing stages, Louth goalkeeper Niall O'Donnell saved well from Ian Robertson; Ciaran Whelan hit the upright and Peter McGinnity and Colin Kelly both scored a point each for the 'Wee County'.

SCORERS – DUBLIN: Declan Darcy 0-5; Ciaran Whelan 0-4; Brendan O'Brien 0-3;
Ian Robertson 1-0; Mick O'Keeffe 1-0; Brian Stynes 0-2; Paddy Christie 0-1
LOUTH: Alan Doherty 0-5; Colin Kelly 0-3; Seamus O'Hanlon 0-2; Aaron Hoey 0-1;
Martin Farrelly 0-1; Cathal O'Hanlon 0-1; Peter McGinnity 0-1

DUBLIN

Davy Byrne

| Paddy Christie | Paddy Moran | Tommo Lynch |
| Paul Curran | Shane Ryan | Keith Galvin |

Ciaran Whelan   Brian Stynes

| Enda Sheehy | Jim Gavin | Declan Darcy |
| Dessie Farrell (Captain) | Ian Roberston | Brendan O'Brien |

SUBSTITUTES: Mick O'Keeffe for Jim Gavin; Darren Homan for Enda Sheehy;
Liam Walsh for Shane Ryan

LOUTH

Niall O'Donnell

| Brien Philips | Gareth O'Neill (Captain) | Simon Gerrard |
| Aaron Hoey | Nicky Malone | Stephen Melia |

Seamus O'Hanlon   Ken Reilly

| Ollie McDonnell | Seán O'Neill | Martin Farrelly |
| David Reilly | Cathal O'Hanlon | Alan Doherty |

SUBSTITUTES: Colin Kelly for Seán O'Neill; Stefan White for Ollie McDonnell;
Peter McGinnity for Aaron Hoey

DUBLIN
BACK ROW L TO R: Enda Sheehy, Ian Robertson, Davy Byrne, Paddy Christie, Brian Stynes, Paddy Moran, Declan Darcy
FRONT ROW L TO R: Brendan O'Brien, Jim Gavin, Shane Ryan, Ciaran Whelan, Dessie Farrell, Keith Galvin, Tommo Lynch, Paul Curran

LOUTH
BACK ROW L TO R: Seamus O'Hanlon, Seán O'Neill, Simon Gerard, Niall O'Donnell, Nicky Malone, Stephen Melia, Ken Reilly
FRONT ROW L TO R: David Reilly, Ollie McDonnell, Aaron Hoey, Gareth O'Neill, Breen Philips, Alan Doherty, Cathal O'Hanlon

SUNDAY, JUNE 13, 1999

LEINSTER SENIOR FOOTBALL CHAMPIONSHIP QUARTER FINAL

LAOIS versus WESTMEATH

CROKE PARK

REFEREE: BRIAN CROWE (CAVAN)

RESULT: LAOIS 1-16 WESTMEATH 1-8

LAOIS PROVED THE UNDOUBTED MASTERS in this quarter final clash against a disappointing Westmeath side that learned the harsh realities of football life in the fast lane. Westmeath, who defeated Carlow and Longford in the previous rounds, found it difficult to cope with the sheer strength, mobility and skill of a highly motivated Laois team.

Laois had the ideal low-key build up to the game whereas a younger and more inexperienced Westmeath team had to contend with much more hype and hysteria following their magnificent All-Ireland Under 21 victory over Kerry. Furthermore, perhaps too much was made of Westmeath's comfortable eleven points win over Longford in the previous round as Laois were always going to provide much more formidable opposition. And so it proved, as Laois advanced to a Leinster semi-final meeting with Dublin by virtue of an eight points victory. Undoubtedly, Westmeath, who have failed to beat Laois in Championship football since 1970, will learn from this experience and come back stronger and more determined in the future. The average age of the team is twenty-three, so there is plenty of reason for optimism within the county. There was always a question mark over the Westmeath back line and Laois certainly exposed frailties that had been disguised somewhat in the games against both Carlow and Longford.

Tony Maher and George Doyle gave Laois a distinct advantage at midfield, particularly in the second half, and this in turn put enormous pressure on the Westmeath back line. The Laois forwards made good use of the generous supply from outfield and picked off some excellent scores. Damien Delaney scored seven points for Laois but there were valuable scoring contributions also from Chris Conway, Ian Fitzgerald and Hughie Emerson.

Not for the first time, Westmeath's star player was Des Dolan, who finished the game as leading scorer with 1-6 but too many of his colleagues failed to deliver on the promise shown in the games against both Carlow and Longford. Dolan, Martin Flanagan and Ger Heavin fared well against the Laois full back line in the first half, but once the supply lines were severed in the second half, it effectively ruled out any chance of a Westmeath victory.

Dolan converted a penalty in the 20th minute, following a foul on Martin Flanagan, and this helped Westmeath into a slender two points lead, 1-5 to 0-6, at the interval. It was obvious in that opening half that Laois, despite playing against the breeze, were winning many of the man to man clashes and their superiority became more pronounced after the break. It was all downhill for Westmeath once Chris Conway scored a fine goal to give Laois a lead they never subsequently relinquished. Westmeath could only score three points in the second half – all from Des Dolan, while Laois swept to victory with some text-book scores, including five points from the in-form Damien Delaney. It was a truly awesome second half display by a Laois side brimming with confidence. The Dubs had better beware!

SCORERS – LAOIS: Damien Delaney 0-7; Chris Conway 1-1; Ian Fitzgerald 0-3; Hughie Emerson 0-2; Kevin Fitzpatrick 0-1; Stephen Kelly 0-1; Tom Kelly 0-1
WESTMEATH: Des Dolan 1-6; Ger Heavin 0-1; Martin Flanagan 0-1

LAOIS

Fergal Byron

Eamonn Delaney   Declan Rooney   Paudge Conway

Derek Conroy   Kevin Fitzpatrick   Joe Higgins

Tony Maher (Captain)   George Doyle

Ian Fitzgerald   Chris Conway   Michael Lawlor

Stephen Kelly   Hughie Emerson   Damien Delaney

SUBSTITUTES: Tom Kelly for Michael Lawlor; Noel Garvan for George Doyle; Greg Ramsbottom for Chris Conway

---

WESTMEATH

Dermot Ryan

Dermot Brady   David Murphy   Fergal Murray

Aidan Lyons   Aidan Canning   Kieran Ryan

Rory O'Connell (Captain)   David O'Shaughnessy

Damien Healy   Mark Staunton   Shane Colleary

Ger Heavin   Martin Flanagan   Des Dolan

SUBSTITUTES: David Mitchell for Aidan Canning; Paul Conway for Aidan Lyons; Michael Ennis for Shane Colleary

LAOIS
BACK ROW L TO R: Chris Conway, Derek Conroy, George Doyle, Declan Rooney, Ian Fitzgerald, Fergal Byron, Kevin Fitzpatrick, Eamonn Delaney, Tony Maher
FRONT ROW: Damien Delaney, Michael Lawlor, Hughie Emerson, Stephen Kelly, Paudge Conway, Joe Higgins

WESTMEATH
BACK ROW L TO R: Aidan Lyons, David Murphy, Mark Staunton, Rory O'Connell, Martin Flanagan, Damien Healy, David O'Shaughnessy
FRONT ROW L TO R: Ger Heavin, Fergal Murray, Shane Colleary, Aidan Canning, Kieran Ryan, Dermot Brady, Des Dolan, Dermot Ryan

SUNDAY, JUNE 13, 1999

LEINSTER SENIOR FOOTBALL CHAMPIONSHIP QUARTER-FINAL

OFFALY versus KILDARE

CROKE PARK

REFEREE: PAT MCENEANEY (MONAGHAN)

RESULT: OFFALY 0-11 KILDARE 0-7

ALTHOUGH JUST FOUR POINTS separated the sides at the finish, Offaly were the more accomplished team on the day and their second half display represented much of what is positive in Gaelic football. Offaly, who lost by twelve points to Meath in last year's Championship, reaped the benefits of a direct style of football against a Kildare side that looked tired at times. A dearth of scoring forwards and a number of injuries to key players also contributed to Kildare's defeat. Offaly played some superb football in the second-half to claim a well merited victory and set up a fascinating semi-final clash with Meath.

Super-fit Offaly took a vice-like grip on the game in the second half and restricted Kildare to a meagre two points on their way to an impressive 0-11 to 0-7 victory. But it would be wrong to just dismiss Kildare's below-par performance without taking into consideration the effect last year's memorable Championship journey had on the players. This current crop of footballers, under the management of Mick O'Dwyer, have restored pride to Kildare football and their wonderful achievement in winning the Leinster title last year for the first time since 1956 will never be forgotten. The energy expended by the players in winning that provincial title and the residue of disappointment following their subsequent defeat by Galway in the All-Ireland Final was bound to take its toll.

Kildare began in sprightly fashion with a point each from play by Karl O'Dwyer and Declan Kerrigan but the scores soon dried up once the Offaly backs knuckled down to the task at hand. Offaly had little luck in front of goal in the early stages. Kildare goalkeeper Christy Byrne proved unbeatable as he brought off a magnificent save from James Stewart and then blocked a follow up effort from Roy Malone in the 4th minute. Malone was also deprived of a goal by a brave block down by Anthony Rainbow. Stewart had another chance of a goal in the 12th minute, but again Christy Byrne brought off a top-class save. The genial Castlemitchell man is unquestionably one of the finest goalkeepers in present day football. Offaly suffered a setback in the 19th minute when wing-back Tom Coffey was injured. Coffey continued to play on for a few minutes until the injury forced him to retire.

All-Star Dermot Earley stretched Kildare's lead with a point from play in the 17th minute by which stage Offaly, incredibly, had still to open their account. But the 1997 Leinster Champions wiped out Kildare's advantage in the space of three minutes: Colm Quinn sent over two frees in quick succession and then Ciaran McManus levelled the game for the first time in the 23rd minute. Both sides continued to spurn chances in the remaining twelve minutes of the first half, during which Karl O'Dwyer pointed two frees for Kildare and Peter Brady scored a point from play for Offaly. Just a point separated the teams at half-time, Kildare 0-5, Offaly 0-4.

Kildare's hopes of victory took a nose-dive early in the second half when Offaly goalkeeper Padraig Kelly brought off two outstanding saves that swung the game decisively in favour of the Midlanders. Kelly blocked a good effort from Willie McCreery in the 40th minute and then pulled off a superb save from Martin Lynch. Had either McCreery or Lynch scored a goal at that stage, then Kildare may have found new life. As it was, Offaly responded with a wonder point from Peter Brady. Championship debutante Barney O'Brien then landed a point to put Offaly ahead for the very first time. Although Martin Lynch responded with a point for Kildare, it soon became apparent that Offaly has established a grip on the game, which they were not about to let slip easily. Finbar Cullen, Vinnie Claffey and Peter Brady scored a point apiece to push Offaly 0-9 to 0-6 in front by the 48th minute. Karl O'Dwyer hit over a free five minutes later to record Kildare's last score of the game. The Offaly defence hustled and harried to such an extent that the Kildare forwards found space at a premium in the second half while James Grennan and Ciaran McManus put in an amount of quality work at midfield. McManus found the target from a '45 and substitute David Connolly wrapped up the scoring with a point from play at the very end of what was a throughly enjoyable Leinster quarter-final.

SCORERS – OFFALY: Peter Brady 0-3; Colm Quinn 0-2; Ciaran McManus 0-2; Barney O'Brien 0-1; Vinnie Claffey 0-1; Finbar Cullen 0-1; David Connolly 0-1;
KILDARE: Karl O'Dwyer 0-4; Declan Kerrigan 0-1; Dermot Earley 0-1; Martin Lynch 0-1

OFFALY

Padraig Kelly

Cathal Daly   Barry Malone   David Foley

John Kenny   Finbar Cullen (Captain)   Tom Coffey

Ciaran McManus   James Grennan

Colm Quinn   Barney O'Brien   James Stewart

Vinnie Claffey   Roy Malone   Peter Brady

SUBSTITUTES: Phil O'Reilly for Tom Coffey; David Connolly for Colm Quinn

KILDARE

Christy Byrne

Brian Lacey   John Finn   Ken Doyle

Derek Maher   Glen Ryan (Captain)   Anthony Rainbow

Paul McCormack   Willie McCreery

Eddie McCormack   Declan Kerrigan   Dermot Earley

Martin Lynch   Karl O'Dwyer   Cathal Sheridan

SUBSTITUTES: Padraig Brennan for Cathal Sheridan; Brian Murphy for Paul McCormack;
Niall Buckley for Brian Murphy

OFFALY
BACK ROW L TO R: John Kenny, Padraig Kelly, Barry Malone, Barney O'Brien, James Grennan, Roy Malone,
Ciaran McManus, Colm Quinn
FRONT ROW L TO R: Peter Brady, James Stewart, Cathal Daly, Finbar Cullen, Vinnie Claffey, David Foley, Tom Coffey

KILDARE
BACK ROW L TO R: Enda Murphy, John Finn, Martin Lynch, Karl O'Dwyer, Willie McCreery, Paul McCormack,
Anthony Rainbow, Ronan Quinn, Derek Maher, Emett Mulhall, Padraig Gravin, John Whelan
FRONT ROW L TO R: Martin Ryan, Ken Doyle, Cathal Sheridan, Brian Lacey, Christy Byrne, Glen Ryan, Declan Kerrigan,
Eddie McCormack, Dermot Earley, Bosco French, Pauric Brennan

SUNDAY, JUNE 27, 1999

LEINSTER SENIOR FOOTBALL CHAMPIONSHIP SEMI-FINAL

DUBLIN versus LAOIS

CROKE PARK

REFEREE: SEAMUS PRIOR (LEITRIM)

RESULT: DUBLIN 1-11 LAOIS 0-14 (A DRAW)

THE TALK AT THE END OF THE GAME was about Ian Robertson's controversial equalising point in injury-time that completed Dublin's magnificent comeback against a superb Laois side that saw victory snatched from their grasp. Rejuvenated Laois appeared to be on the brink of a first Championship win over Dublin since 1981 when a point from play by Hughie Emerson pushed them 0-14 to 0-10 ahead with little more than one minute of normal time remaining. But Dublin displayed tremendous character to fight back and force a draw in dramatic circumstances. Firstly, Ian Robertson scored a superb goal after latching on to a pass from Ciaran Whelan before despatching the ball past Laois goalkeeper Fergal Byron. And then came that much-talked about equaliser! Robertson, a player of genuine class, got on the end of a pass from Jason Sherlock and fisted the ball over the bar to level the game. The Ballymun Kickhams player appeared to pick the ball off the ground but referee Seamus Prior allowed the score to stand and Dublin players and supporters breathed a sigh of relief. Credit both teams for their part in what was a magnificent game that produced many memorable moments. Laois recovered from a six-point deficit early on to dictate the pace for long stages before Dublin rallied late on to take a share of the spoils.

There was no stopping rampant Dublin in the opening quarter and the scores mounted as the Laois defence struggled to cope with the onslaught. Wing-back Keith Galvin and midfielder Brian Stynes kicked over the opening points as Dublin, with wind advantage, established a firm grip on the game very early on. Declan Darcy then decided to make his mark by kicking two magnificent points – one off his left foot, the other off his right, as Dublin threatened to run riot. Ian Robertson scored Dublin's fifth point from play while Jim Gavin converted a free in the 16th minute to become the fifth player to score for the Dubs.

Tony Maher opened the scoring for Laois in the 17th minute and that score was quickly followed by a pointed free from Ian Fitzgerald. The introduction of Michael Lawlor in place of Chris Conway in the 21st minute proved an inspirational substitution by manager Tom Cribben. Lawlor made an immediate impact as he tore at the Dublin defence with single-minded determination. Stephen Kelly reduced the margin still further with a point from play as Laois began to dictate the pace. David Sweeney replaced Tom Kelly in the 26th minute as Laois lifted the pace appreciably. Laois were now on top at midfield; their defence tightened up considerably and many Dublin moves floundered through tenacious defending by the

Laois backs. In a period of sustained dominance by Laois, Damien Delaney scored three points from frees to level the game for the first time in the 31st minute.

Although Dublin replied with a pointed free by Jim Gavin and a superb effort from play by Dessie Farrell, it was Laois who remained in control. Tony Maher shot wide with a goal at his mercy while Stephen Kelly scored the final point of the opening half to leave the game delicately poised at the interval, Dublin 0-8, Laois 0-7.

Michael Lawlor levelled the match for the second time mere seconds after the re-start and he continued to have a major influence with his determined play. David Sweeney, too, contributed handsomely and his two points from play together with a point apiece from Hughie Emerson and Damien Delaney helped Laois into a 0-12 to 0-9 lead by the 56th minute. Earlier, Dublin suffered a setback when Paul Curran had to retire injured with a broken collarbone.

Dublin had a wonderful opportunity to level the game when the referee awarded a penalty after he adjudged that Declan Rooney had fouled Ian Robertson. Paddy Christie made the journey from his full back position to take the kick, which was brilliantly tipped over the crossbar by Laois goalkeeper Fergal Byron. Dublin missed numerous scoring chances – no less than 12 second half wides - and their Championship appeared to be over for another year when Damien Delaney and Hughie Emerson scored a point each, but Robertson saved the day with a fine goal and that controversial point. Drama to the very end!

SCORERS – DUBLIN: Ian Robertson 1-2; Jim Gavin 0-3; Declan Darcy 0-2; Dessie Farrell 0-1; Keith Galvin 0-1; Brian Stynes 0-1; Paddy Christie 0-1
LAOIS: Damien Delaney 0-5; Hughie Emerson 0-2; Stephen Kelly 0-2; David Sweeney 0-2; Ian Fitzgerald 0-1; Tony Maher 0-1; Michael Lawlor 0-1

DUBLIN

Davy Byrne

Paddy Moran	Paddy Christie	Tommo Lynch
Paul Croft	Paul Curran	Keith Galvin

Ciaran Whelan   Brian Stynes

Enda Sheehy	Jim Gavin	Declan Darcy
Dessie Farrell (Captain)	Ian Robertson	Brendan O'Brien

SUBSTITUTES: Jason Sherlock for Brendan O'Brien; Darren Homan for Brian Stynes; Shane Ryan for Paul Curran

---

LAOIS

Fergal Byron

Eamonn Delaney   Declan Rooney   Paudge Conway

Derek Conroy   Kevin Fitzpatrick   Joe Higgins

Tony Maher (Captain)   George Doyle

Ian Fitzgerald   Hughie Emerson   Tom Kelly

Stephen Kelly   Damien Delaney   Chris Conway

SUBSTITUTES: Michael Lawlor for Chris Conway; David Sweeney for Tom Kelly; Greg Ramsbottom for Ian Fitzgerald

DUBLIN
BACK ROW L TO R: Enda Sheehy, Ian Robertson, Paddy Christie, Brian Stynes, Paddy Moran, Paul Croft
FRONT ROW L TO R: Paul Curran, Jim Gavin, Brendan O'Brien, Davy Byrne, Dessie Farrell, Ciaran Whelan, Keith Galvin, Tommo Lynch, Declan Darcy

LAOIS
BACK ROW L TO R: Chris Conway, Derek Conroy, Ian Fitzgerald, Fergal Byron, Kevin Fitzpatrick, Eamonn Delaney, George Doyle, Tony Maher
FRONT ROW L TO R: Damien Delaney, Hughie Emerson, Declan Rooney, Stephen Kelly, Paudge Conway, Joe Higgins, Tom Kelly

SUNDAY, JULY 4, 1999

LEINSTER SENIOR FOOTBALL CHAMPIONSHIP SEMI-FINAL

MEATH versus OFFALY

CROKE PARK

REFEREE: MICHAEL CURLEY (GALWAY)

RESULT: MEATH 1-13 OFFALY 0-9

THE MESSAGE FROM CROKE PARK was loud and clear and only the foolish would choose to ignore it! Beware! Meath are back and looking good, very good indeed! Seán Boylan's team produced a powerful second half display that Offaly simply could not match on the day. Meath were physically stronger in key areas and that combined with their mobility, skill and awesome work-rate ensured Offaly were continually chasing the game. Typically, Offaly gave their all in an attempt to retrieve the situation in the second half, but were given little leeway by a strong and forceful Meath team in what was a very physically demanding game. The Meath full back line of Mark O'Reilly, the inspirational Darren Fay, until his retirement through injury late in the game, and Cormac Murphy dominated their patch and rarely gave an inch to Vinnie Claffey, Roy Malone or Peter Brady. The Meath half-back line was also impressive and consequently Offaly's scores dried up in the second half. Indeed the 1997 Leinster Champions, could only score two points, both from placed kicks in a second half that Meath dominated. John McDermott shone at midfield with good assistance from Nigel Crawford while Ollie Murphy and Tommy Dowd tormented the Offaly defence. Meath goalkeeper Cormac Sullivan more than played his part in the victory and brought off a superb save in the 26th minute to deny Offaly wing-forward Barney O'Brien a goal and he also saved a good effort from Vinnie Claffey in the second half. Offaly goalkeeper Padraig Kelly also displayed his agility when he saved brilliantly from Hank Traynor in the 59th minute.

It was a very competitive and evenly matched first half that produced ten scores from play and some wonderful passages of hard honest to goodness football. The sides were level, 0-7 apiece, at the interval but, even at that stage, it was evident that Offaly, although favoured by the breeze, were finding it difficult to cope with the strong running and die-for-the-next-ball endeavour of the Meath men. Offaly played their best football in that opening half and midfielder Ciaran McManus was somewhat unfortunate at the start when he bounded forward to score a point from a powerful shot that could easily have resulted in a goal. It was a warning signal for Meath and the defence was never as vulnerable thereafter. David Connolly increased Offaly's lead with a pointed free but then excellent scores from play by Tommy Dowd, Donal Curtis and Evan Kelly left Meath ahead for the first time after sixteen minutes play. Connolly was again on the mark from a free to level the match but a point each from Ollie Murphy and Trevor Giles gave Meath a two points cushion. Barry Malone, John Kenny, Finbar Cullen and Ciaran McManus initiated many good moves as Offaly regained their early sparkle and sprinted clear with a flurry of points from James Grennan, James Stewart, Peter Brady and David Connolly. But the first half ended with Seán Boylan's team in the ascendancy, courtesy of points from Graham Geraghty, who became the sixth Meath forward to score, and the mighty Tommy Dowd from Dunderry.

Meath won an abundance of possession early in the second half but failed miserably to take the scoring chances that came their way and shot six wides before eventually finding the target. Seán Boylan told me afterwards that he was concerned about his team's wayward marksmanship early in the second half, especially when Ciaran McManus kicked a magnificent point to edge Offaly in front. But Meath took control from the time Tommy Dowd sent over the equalising point and Ollie Murphy crashed the ball to the net following a sweeping move. Vinnie Claffey appeared to be fouled during an Offaly attack but the referee allowed the play to go on. John McDermott delivered a high ball, which was gathered by Graham Geraghty, who sprinted clear before passing to Murphy for the crucial goal. That score deflated Offaly and with Tommy Dowd and Ollie Murphy in sparkling form, Meath pulled away in the closing quarter to book their place in the Leinster Final.

Afterwards, that marvellous ambassador of Gaelic Football, Tommy Lyons, who guided Offaly to a Leinster title and League success, announced he was stepping down as manager, citing the enormous amount of time now required to do the job.

SCORERS – MEATH: Ollie Murphy 1-3; Tommy Dowd 0-4; Trevor Giles 0-3; Donal Curtis 0-1; Evan Kelly 0-1; Graham Geraghty 0-1
OFFALY: David Connolly 0-3; Ciaran McManus 0-2; Vinnie Claffey 0-1; James Grennan 0-1; James Stewart 0-1; Peter Brady 0-1

MEATH

Cormac Sullivan

Mark O'Reilly	Darren Fay	Cormac Murphy
Paddy Reynolds	Enda McManus	Hank Traynor

Nigel Crawford   John McDermott

Evan Kelly	Trevor Giles	Donal Curtis
Ollie Murphy	Graham Geraghty (Captain)	Tommy Dowd

SUBSTITUTES: Nigel Nestor for Evan Kelly; Richie Kealy for Darren Fay

Padraig Kelly

Cathal Daly   Barry Malone   David Foley

John Kenny   Finbar Cullen (Captain)   Tom Coffey

Ciaran McManus   James Grennan

James Stewart   Barney O'Brien   David Connolly

Vinnie Claffey   Roy Malone   Peter Brady

SUBSTITUTES: Ronan Mooney for David Connolly; Seán Grennan for Barney O'Brien; Phil O'Reilly for David Foley

MEATH
BACK ROW L TO R: Trevor Giles, John McDermott, Graham Geraghty, Darren Fay, Cormac Sullivan, Nigel Crawford, Hank Traynor, Cormac Murphy
FRONT ROW L TO R: Mark O'Reilly, Evan Kelly, Donal Curtis, Tommy Dowd, Paddy Reynolds, Ollie Murphy, Enda McManus

OFFALY
BACK ROW L TO R: Barney O'Brien, John Kenny, James Stewart, Padraig Kelly, James Grennan, Roy Malone, Ciaran McManus
FRONT ROW L TO R: Peter Brady, Cathal Daly, David Connolly, Finbar Cullen, Barry Malone, Vinnie Claffey, David Foley, Tom Coffey

SUNDAY, JULY 18, 1999

LEINSTER SENIOR FOOTBALL CHAMPIONSHIP SEMI-FINAL (REPLAY)

DUBLIN versus LAOIS

CROKE PARK

REFEREE: SEAMUS PRIOR (LEITRIM)

RESULT: DUBLIN 0-16 LAOIS 1-11

IT IS NEVER WISE TO GIVE DUBLIN a second chance as Laois learned to their cost in this replay, which produced far less quality football than in the drawn encounter, but which nevertheless lacked nothing in excitement and endeavour. Laois suffered the misfortune of having their free-taker Damien Delaney dismissed at the end of the first half for a foul on Paul Croft. Referee Seamus Prior called Delaney aside and promptly produced the red card much to the dismay of the Laois corner forward who vehemently protested his innocence. But Prior was adamant the Laois man was guilty of a sending off offence and no amount of arguing was going to change his mind. Dublin led by four points at half-time and had doubled that advantage within fourteen minutes of the re-start with a point from Enda Sheehy and three in a row from the impressive Declan Darcy. Reduced to fourteen players and eight points in arrears, Laois were faced with two options: throw in the towel and suffer annihilation or put their shoulders to the wheel and take the fight to the Dubs. To their credit, Tom Cribben's team chose the latter option and stormed back into the game.

Ian Fitzgerald scored a point from a free in the 50th minute and spirited Laois came alive when Chris Conway fired over a point. A short time earlier, Laois goalkeeper, Fergal Byron brilliantly blocked a first-timed effort from Jason Sherlock. Full-forward Ian Robertson, who along with Brian Stynes, produced a stunning display, scored his fourth point from play, to push Dublin, 0-14 to 0-7, ahead. Somehow from a clear winning position, the Dubs lost their way, becoming less assured and more disjointed with each passing minute. Fourteen-man Laois sensed the Dubs were in distress and took full advantage of their edginess. Hughie Emerson was a man inspired in the last quarter as Dublin were put to the pin of their collar to survive. Emerson was a revelation and scored two magnificent points from play while Ian Fitzgerald pointed two frees. Laois were now just three points in arrears, but when the need was greatest, Brian Stynes stepped into the breach and scored two great points. But Laois were far from finished and Chris Conway converted a penalty in injury-time – a low shot to the corner of the net, to cut the deficit to just two points. It was a close call for Dublin and their manager Tommy Carr said later, "It was not the perfect performance, but we didn't need the perfect performance today."

Ian Roberston and Brian Stynes shone brightest for Dublin. Stynes, substituted in the drawn game, was simply magnificent all through and his high fielding and work-rate were central to the Dubs success. The Ballyboden/St. Enda's club man also scored three points from play in one of his best ever displays for the county. Robertston, too, was a sensation, scoring four points from play and creating numerous other scores. The sides were level, 0-5 apiece, after 20 minutes with Robertson scoring two points for Dublin and the in-form Stephen Kelly accounting for the same total for Laois. Kelly gave Tommo Lynch a torrid time, forcing Dublin manager Tommy Carr to bring in Peadar Andrews as early as the 20th minute in an attempt to curb the St. Joseph's player. Andrews played exceptionally well and Kelly was never as effective thereafter.

Dublin hit the front with four unanswered points from Darcy, Stynes, Robertson and Dessie Farrell to establish a 0-9 to 0-5 advantage at the break. Dublin mixed the very good with the bad in the second half as Laois recovered from that eight point deficit to close the gap to just two points at the finish.

SCORERS – DUBLIN: Declan Darcy 0-5; Ian Robertson 0-4; Brian Stynes 0-3; Dessie Farrell 0-1; Ciaran Whelan 0-1; Enda Sheehy 0-1; Jim Gavin 0-1
LAOIS: Ian Fitzgerald 0-4; Chris Conway 1-1; Stephen Kelly 0-2; Damien Delaney 0-2; Hughie Emerson 0-2;

DUBLIN

Davy Byrne

Paddy Moran   Paddy Chrisite   Tommo Lynch

Paul Croft   Jonathan McGee   Keith Galvin

Ciaran Whelan   Brian Stynes

Enda Sheehy   Dessie Farrell (Captain)   Declan Darcy

Jim Gavin   Ian Robertson   Jason Sherlock

SUBSTITUTES: Peadar Andrews for Tommo Lynch; Darren Homan for Enda Sheehy; Niall O'Donoghue for Ian Robertson

LAOIS

Fergal Byron

Eamonn Delaney   Declan Rooney   Paudge Conway

Derek Conroy   Kevin Fitzpatrick   Joe Higgins

Tony Maher (Captain)   George Doyle

Ian Fitzgerald   Hughie Emerson   David Sweeney

Stephen Kelly   Michael Lawlor   Damien Delaney

SUBSTITUTES: Noel Garvan for Declan Rooney ; Chris Conway for David Sweeney; Brian 'Beano' McDonald for Michael Lawlor

DUBLIN
BACK ROW L TO R: Davy Byrne, Enda Sheehy, Ian Robertson, Paul Croft, Paddy Christie, Brian Stynes, Jonathan McGee, Paddy Moran
FRONT ROW L TO R: Jason Sherlock, Jim Gavin, Ciaran Whelan, Dessie Farrell, Keith Galvin, Tommo Lynch, Declan Darcy

LAOIS
BACK ROW L TO R: David Sweeney, Derek Conroy, Ian Fitzgerald, Fergal Byron, Kevin Fitzpatrick, Eamonn Delaney, George Doyle, Tony Maher, Michael Lawlor
FRONT ROW L TO R: Damien Delaney, Declan Rooney, Hughie Emerson, Stephen Kelly, Paudge Conway, Joe Higgins

SUNDAY, AUGUST 1, 1999

LEINSTER SENIOR FOOTBALL CHAMPIONSHIP FINAL

MEATH versus DUBLIN

CROKE PARK

REFEREE: MICHAEL CURLEY (GALWAY)

RESULT: MEATH 1-14 DUBLIN 0-12

IN A FEW YEARS TIME IT WILL SURELY become known as the Ollie Murphy Final! The dynamic Carnaross man was the outstanding player on view in this the forty-fourth meeting of Meath and Dublin in the Championship. One had to feel sympathy for Dublin corner back Peadar Andrews who found it impossible to cope with the speed and clinical finishing of the in-form Murphy, who scored no less than 1-5 from play.

Dublin manager Tommy Carr and his selectors were criticised afterwards for leaving Andrews so exposed for sixty minutes when it was evident early on that the St. Brigid's player was struggling to contain the rampaging Murphy. To be fair to Andrews, it has to be said than any player would have found it difficult to curb the threat of Murphy, such was his devastating form on the day.

Trevor Giles, who missed two eminently scorable frees early on, was another player who contributed handsomely to Meath's win. The '1996 Footballer of the Year' won an amount of breaking ball and as always distributed it to telling effect. Apart from scoring five points, the influential Giles was also involved in many of the other Meath scores and it was his sublime cross-field foot pass that set up Ollie Murphy for the clinching goal in the 59th minute. Interestingly, centre-half-back Jonathan McGee fared well early on but the determined Giles went on to have a major impact on the game. The Meath defence, apart from a few shaky moments, was strong and assured, and confined the Dublin attack to just two points from play – both from Jim Gavin, while the other point from play came from impressive midfielder, Ciaran Whelan. Admittedly, Dublin lost their captain Dessie Farrell through injury after just sixteen minutes play and his departure considerably weakened the attack. Meath centre-half-back Enda McManus had to retire injured in the 19th minute but Meath adjusted well to the setback. John McDermott, whose mother sadly died a week before the game, put in an enormous amount of hard work throughout the field and played a major role in Meath's victory. But most of all, Meath's success was built around a supreme team effort where every single player competed vigorously for seventy minutes. Meath forward, Tommy Dowd underwent an operation on his back the day before the game, but still turned up in Croke Park to urge on his teammates.

Ciaran Whelan was outstanding at midfield for Dublin and his superb point from play in the 50th minute closed the gap to just two points. Jim Gavin fired over another point from play but Ollie Murphy's goal less than ten minutes later set Meath on the way to a nineteenth Leinster crown.

Playing with the breeze, Dublin came close to scoring a goal after just four minutes play but Meath goalkeeper Cormac Sullivan brilliantly blocked Jason Sherlock's shot. Nine minutes later, Meath corner forward Evan Kelly was denied a certain goal with an equally impressive block by Dublin goalkeeper Davy Byrne. By that stage, Meath had moved 0-2 to 0-1 ahead through points from play by Graham Geraghty and Ollie Murphy. Jim Gavin had opened the scoring for Dublin with a pointed free in the seventh minute. Dublin won an abundance of possession in the opening quarter but failed to get the scores that might have changed the course of the game. As it was, the Dubs trailed at the interval by two points, having failed to break down a resolute Meath defence. Meath scored four of their six first half points from play – two from Murphy and one each from Geraghty and Nigel Nestor- to Dublin's solitary point from play by Gavin, who also scored two points from placed kicks. Declan Darcy accounted for Dublin's other point from a free while Trevor Giles found the target with two frees for Meath.

Declan Darcy was on the mark for Dublin within 30 seconds of the re-start when he pointed a free but Meath continued to hold the upperhand primarily because of their ability to score points from play.

Murphy and Hank Traynor – the fifth Meath player to score – sent over a point each from play; Darcy pointed a free in reply before Giles scored his first point from play to push

Meath 0-9 to 0-6 ahead.

Even though Ciaran Whelan and Jim Gavin kicked two fine points from play, Giles and Murphy once again combined to turn the tide in favour of the Royal County. Murphy scored 1-2 in a three-minute spell to effectively seal Dublin's fate. Dublin scored four points from frees in the closing ten minutes – three from Darcy and one from Gavin – while Meath's brace of points in that same period came from Giles and captain Graham Geraghty

SCORERS – MEATH: Ollie Murphy 1-5; Trevor Giles 0-5; Graham Geraghty 0-2; Nigel Nestor 0-1; Hank Traynor 0-1
DUBLIN: Declan Darcy 0-6; Jim Gavin 0-5; Ciaran Whelan 0-1

MEATH

Cormac Sullivan

| Mark O'Reilly | Darren Fay | Cormac Murphy |
| Hank Traynor | Enda McManus | Paddy Reynolds |

Nigel Crawford   John McDermott

| Evan Kelly | Trevor Giles | Nigel Nestor |
| Ollie Murphy | Graham Geraghty (Captain) | Donal Curtis |

SUBSTITUTES: Richie Kealy for Enda McManus;

DUBLIN

Davy Byrne

| Keith Galvin | Paddy Christie | Peadar Andrews |
| Paul Croft | Jonathan McGee | Paddy Moran |

Ciaran Whelan   Brian Stynes

| Enda Sheehy | Dessie Farrell (Captain) | Declan Darcy |
| Jim Gavin | Ian Robertson | Jason Sherlock |

SUBSTITUTES: Ray Cosgrove for Dessie Farrell; Darren Homan for Ray Cosgrove;
Peter Ward for Enda Sheehy

MEATH
BACK ROW L TO R: Trevor Giles, John McDermott, Graham Geraghty, Darren Fay, Cormac Sullivan, Nigel Crawford, Hank Traynor, Nigel Nestor, Cormac Murphy
FRONT ROW L TO R: Mark O'Reilly, Donal Curtis, Evan Kelly, Ollie Murphy, Paddy Reynolds, Enda McManus

DUBLIN
BACK ROW L TO R: Enda Sheehy, Ian Robertson, Davy Byrne, Peadar Andrews, Paddy Christie, Paul Croft, Brian Stynes, Jonathan McGee, Paddy Moran
FRONT ROW L TO R: Jason Sherlock, Jim Gavin, Ciaran Whelan, Dessie Farrell, Keith Galvin, Declan Darcy

SUNDAY, MAY 23, 1999

MUNSTER SENIOR FOOTBALL CHAMPIONSHIP

CORK versus WATERFORD

FRAHER FIELD (DUNGARVAN)

REFEREE: AIDAN MANGAN (KERRY)

RESULT: CORK 3-23 WATERFORD 0-4

ONE HAD TO FEEL SYMPATHY FOR WATERFORD footballers after they suffered a humiliating twenty-eight point drubbing at the hands of the League Champions Cork in a game that served little purpose for either side. I was covering the match in Fraher Field for RTE Radio Sport and it had many similarities with the game the previous evening at Semple Stadium, which I also attended, between the hurlers of Tipperary and Kerry. Newly crowned League hurling champions Tipperary trounced Kerry by a staggering twenty-nine points at Semple Stadium while the current League football champions Cork easily defeated Waterford by twenty-eight points. Furthermore, Kerry hurlers and Waterford footballers only scored a solitary point in the second half and were each outscored in that totally one-sided second period by much superior opposition by twenty-two points. It is now time for a re-think! Any system would be preferable to the one, which allows teams suffer such demoralising defeats as those endured by Tipperary hurlers and Waterford footballers.

Waterford were completely out of their depth against a far superior Cork side and, needless to say, such an annihilation does nothing but damage the morale of the players concerned. Waterford footballers put a tremendous amount of work into their preparation but, despite their gallant efforts, the gulf in class was too much against a team of Cork's undoubted pedigree. Waterford manager, John Cummins, father of Tipperary dual star, Brendan, spoke to me afterwards live on RTE Radio One and suggested that one way forward was to have a round robin system for weaker counties.

Although playing against a stiff breeze, Cork led by 0-9 to 0-3 at the interval with Philip Clifford and Damien O'Neill scoring three points apiece for the visitors. Martin Power scored two points for Waterford while Richie Power landed the final point of the opening half. Waterford could have been closer at the break but for the fact that a number of scorable frees were sent wide. Although Waterford displayed commendable character in that opening half and competed for every ball, it was evident Cork were the superior team. It was patently obvious at the break that Waterford were facing a very heavy defeat but it turned out to be even worse than anticipated. To compound their problems, Waterford were reduced to fourteen players in the 49th minute when full-back George Walsh was shown the red card for a second bookable offence.

Waterford could only manage a single point from youngster Garry Hurney for their second half efforts while rampant Cork scored 3-14 with some awesome forward play. Cork never let up and continued to pile on the scores even though the game was over as a contest at half-time. Competition for places on the Cork team has never been keener and no player wants to display any level of complacency in case someone else is called on to fill his shoes. It was no more than target practice at the finish, as the game petered out to its inevitable conclusion. Cork picked off points with consummate ease while their goals came from Mark O'Sullivan, Damien O'Neill and wing-forward Aidan Dorgan. Cork's tally of 3-23 was the highest recorded in the 1999 Football Championship while Waterford's 0-4 was the lowest!

SCORERS – CORK: Damien O'Neill 1-5; Mark O'Sullivan 1-4; Joe Kavanagh 0-5; Aidan Dorgan 1-2; Philip Clifford 0-4; Ciarán O'Sullivan 0-2; Don Davis 0-1
WATERFORD: Martin Power 0-2; Richie Power 0-1; Garry Hurney 0-1

CORK

Kevin O'Dwyer

Michael O'Donovan	Seán Óg Ó hAilpín	Anthony Lynch
Ciarán O'Sullivan	Ronan McCarthy	Martin Cronin

Nicholas Murphy   Micheál O'Sullivan

Aidan Dorgan	Joe Kavanagh	Don Davis
Philip Clifford	Damien O'Neill (Captain)	Mark O'Sullivan

SUBSTITUTES: Fachtna Collins for Nicholas Murphy; Alan O'Regan for Philip Clifford; John Miskella for Ciarán O'Sullivan

---

WATERFORD

Ciaran Cotter

Jason Crotty	George Walsh	Mattie Kiely
Ciarán Whelan	Lawrence Hurney	Liam Dalton

Aidan Aherne   William Kavanagh

Michael O'Brien (Captain)	Richie Power	Colin Keane
Garry Hurney	Martin Power	Michael Downey

SUBSTITUTES: Eoin Hartery for Michael O'Brien; Don McMahon for Michael Downey

CORK
BACK ROW L TO R: Nicholas Murphy, Philip Clifford, Mihéal O'Sullivan, Damien O'Neill, Ronan McCarthy, Mark O'Sullivan, Ciarán O'Sullivan
FRONT ROW L TO R: Anthony Lynch, Kevin O'Dwyer, Don Davis, Joe Kavanagh, Michael O'Donovan, Martin Cronin, Seán Óg Ó hAilpín, Aidan Dorgan

WATERFORD
BACK ROW L TO R: : Martin Power, Michael O'Brien, Lawrence Hurney, Aidan Ahearne, Kieran Cotter, William Kavanagh, Kieran Whelan, Colin Keane, Jason Crotty
FRONT ROW L TO R: Garry Hurney, Liam Dalton, Richie Power, Mattie Kiely, Michael Downey, George Walsh

SUNDAY, MAY 23, 1999

MUNSTER SENIOR FOOTBALL CHAMPIONSHIP

KERRY versus TIPPERARY

AUSTIN STACK PARK (TRALEE)

REFEREE: MICHAEL COLLINS (CORK)

RESULT: KERRY 1-11 TIPPERARY 0-8

How can a wide possibly become a goal? That was the question everyone was asking following a bizarre incident barely eight minutes into this high-tension, first-round clash at Austin Stack Park.

Kerry corner-forward Gerry Murphy clearly kicked the ball wide but it came back into play off a stanchion and the Rathmore player finished the rebound to the net. Furious Tipperary defenders protested long and hard but to no avail. Cork referee, Michael Collins, consulted his umpires and the 'goal', was allowed stand. As television pictures had clearly revealed that the ball had gone wide, Munster Council Chairman, Seán Kelly, a Kerryman, informed the referee at half-time of Tipperary's anger at the decision to allow a goal following a protest from their Football Board Chairman Michael Frawley. But there was to be no change of mind. Subsequently, the Munster Council turned down Tipperary's appeal for a replay. Chairman Seán Kelly apologised to Tipperary for what he described as a 'human error'.

Kerry failed to score from two penalty kicks in the second half but recovered their composure to produce a storming finish which yielded five points in the closing eight minutes in reply to Tipperary's solitary score in the same period. Kerry played some top class football in the first half but were really put to the pin of their collar after the break as a rejuvenated Tipperary, searching for their first Championship victory over the Kingdom since 1928, threatened to pull off a shock victory. Of serious concern to manager, Páidí Ó Sé, was the fact that Kerry failed to register a single score from the 29th to the 62nd minute, during which time Tipperary hit over five points.

1997 All-Ireland winning captain, Liam Hassett, had to withdraw from the Kerry team because of injury before the start and was replaced by Championship newcomer Aodán MacGearailt, who more than impressed with three points from play. With a strong breeze behind them, Kerry had built up an interval advantage of six points, 1-6 to 0-3, but there were indications before the break that Tipperary's challenge was beginning to take shape. There was a long delay before Tipperary eventually reappeared for the second half by which time an official protest had been lodged.

The trend of the game changed dramatically from very early in the second half. All-Star Declan Browne pointed a free and a Peter Lambert point from play followed. Browne, untypically off target on a number of occasions throughout the game, sent over a fine point from play, as a highly motivated Tipperary fought their way back in determined style. Then came the first Kerry penalty after Dara Ó Cinnéide was fouled by Benny Hahessy after a fine Kerry move. However, Maurice Fitzgerald's kick was well saved by Tipperary goalkeeper, Philly Ryan. There was more drama soon afterwards when Kerry were awarded a second penalty. But again no luck for Kerry as Dara Ó Cinnéide sent the ball wide. Those two penalty misses would have rocked any team to the core but Kerry kept their composure and played their way back into the game, helped in no small way by the fact that Tipperary missed a number of excellent chances. There was a hint of a shock when Declan Browne cut the deficit to a mere two points but the tide turned once Maurice Fitzgerald converted a '45 in the 62nd minute to open Kerry's second half account. It was to prove a crucial score. The highly impressive Seamus Moynihan, outstanding throughout the game, then set up Aodán MacGearailt for a fine score while substitute Billy O'Shea, who came on in place of John McGlynn, put Kerry further ahead with a point from play. Kerry defender, Eamonn Breen, was then sent off for a second bookable offence following a foul on Davy Hogan. Even though Damien Byrne replied with a point for Tipperary to close the gap to four points, Kerry were now in the driving seat and Fitzgerald landed two more points to secure victory in a game that will forever be remembered for the Kerry goal that never was!

SCORERS – KERRY: Maurice Fitzgerald 0-4; Aodán MacGearailt 0-3; Gerry Murphy 1-0; Noel Kennelly 0-1; John McGlynn 0-1; Billy O'Shea 0-1; Dara Ó Sé 0-1
TIPPERARY: Declan Browne 0-4; Peter Lambert 0-2; Seán Maher 0-1; Damien Byrne 0-1

KERRY

Declan O'Keeffe

Michael McCarthy   Barry O'Shea   Killian Burns

Tomás Ó Sé   Seamus Moynihan (Captain)   Eamonn Breen

Dara Ó Sé   Donal Daly

John McGlynn   Noel Kennelly   Dara Ó Cinnéide

Gerry Murphy   Aodán MacGearailt   Maurice Fitzgerald

SUBSTITUTES: Billy O'Shea for John McGlynn; Brian Clarke for Gerry Murphy

---

TIPPERARY

Philly Ryan

Conor O'Dwyer   Niall Kelly   Liam Cronin

Benny Hahessy   Seán Collum   Damien Byrne

John Costello   Derry Foley

Seán Maher   Davy Hogan   Des Lyons

Peter Lambert   Mark Sheahan   Declan Browne (Captain)

SUBSTITUTES: Conor O'Shea for Mark Sheahan; James Williams for Des Lyons

KERRY
BACK ROW L TO R: Dara Ó Sé, Barry O' Shea, Maurice Fitzgerald, Noel Kennelly, John McGlynn, Donal Daly, Tomás Ó Sé, Aodán Mac Gearailt
FRONT ROW L TO R: Killian Burns, Michael McCarthy, Dara Ó Cinneide, Declan O'Keeffe, Seamus Moynihan, Gerry Murphy, Eamonn Breen

TIPPERARY
BACK ROW L TO R: Damien Byrne, Niall Kelly, John Costello, Derry Foley, Seán Maher, Conor O'Dwyer, Des Lyons, Mark Sheahan
FRONT ROW L TO R: Peter Lambert, Declan Browne, Philly Ryan, Davy Hogan, Seán Collum, Benny Hahessy, Liam Cronin

SATURDAY, JUNE 19, 1999

MUNSTER SENIOR FOOTBALL CHAMPIONSHIP SEMI-FINAL

CORK versus LIMERICK

PÁIRC UÍ RINN

REFEREE: SEAMUS MC CORMACK (MEATH)

RESULT: CORK 4-13 LIMERICK 1-6

THE FINAL SCORELINE IS GROSSLY UNFAIR to a brave and committed Limerick side that certainly kept Cork on their toes in the first half but were unable to make any significant impact after the break. There was no doubting Cork's superiority in the second half as Larry Tompkins' team outscored Limerick by 2-11 to 0-4 to emerge clear winners by sixteen points. It is always a pleasure to visit Páirc Uí Rinn for any game and I thoroughly enjoyed the atmosphere on this occasion. The officials are always very courteous and efficient and their professional approach ensures that everything runs smoothly.

The game itself was lively and entertaining, particularly in the first half, in the course of which Limerick played some outstanding football and only trailed by a goal at the interval. It all began to go terribly wrong for Limerick after Joe Kavanagh scored a superb individual goal in the 43rd minute to put Cork 3-3 to 1-3 ahead. That goal rocked Limerick and completely altered the course of the game. From there to the finish, Cork took control and played some exhibition football on the way to their expected victory. Midfielder John Quane was to the fore in many excellent Limerick moves and the Galtee Gaels man scored a fine point for good measure early in the second half.

Podsie O'Mahony and Noel Mulvihill swapped points early on before Alan O'Regan scored the opening goal of the game when he palmed the ball to the net past Eamonn Scollard. Michael Reidy replied with a point for Limerick but the visitors soon suffered another blow when the impressive Podsie O'Mahony crashed the ball to the net. But Limerick's perseverance was rewarded when Michael Reidy converted a penalty after seventeen minutes to reduce the deficit to just two points.

It was to be Limerick's last score of the first half while Cork fared little better with just a point from Joe Kavanagh in twenty-one minutes play up to half-time. Both defences played superbly in the first half and signs on them, as Cork registered just four scores to Limerick's three. Cork were mediocre at times in that first half but there was a vast improvement in their general play after the break as the players moved the ball with speed in slippery conditions. Cork led by 2-2 to 1-2 at half-time and the League Champions increased their lead with a point by Mark O'Sullivan within 45 seconds of the re-start.

Limerick full-forward Noel Mulvihill missed a golden chance of a goal in the 38th minute when he inexplicably kicked wide in front of an open goal. It was cruel luck on the talented Mulvihill and it was evident Limerick's cause was lost when Kavanagh scored a vital goal for Cork. Podsie O'Mahony was now in full flight and the Ballincollig man added a further eight points to his tally before match end to bring his total to 1-9. Substitute Fionán Murray scored Cork's fourth goal with four minutes remaining to complete Limerick's misery. It must be said that Limerick have improved immeasurably under the management of Paddy Mulvihill and surely there are better days ahead for this young team around the football fields of Munster.

SCORERS – CORK: Podsie O'Mahony 1-9; Joe Kavanagh 1-2; Fionán Murray 1-0; Alan O'Regan 1-0; Mark O'Sullivan 0-1; Aidan Dorgan 0-1
SCORERS – LIMERICK: Michael Reidy 1-2; Noel Mulvihill 0-1; John Quane 0-1; Michael O'Doherty 0-1; Derek Ryan 0-1

CORK

Kevin O'Dwyer

Ronan McCarthy   Seán Óg Ó hAilpín   Anthony Lynch

Ciarán O'Sullivan   Eoin Sexton   Martin Cronin

Nicholas Murphy   Micheál O'Sullivan

Aidan Dorgan   Joe Kavanagh   Podsie O'Mahony

Mark O'Sullivan   Damien O'Neill (Captain)   Alan O'Regan

SUBSTITUTES: Fionán Murray for Damien O'Neill; Don Davis for Alan O'Regan;
Fachtna Collins for Micheál O'Sullivan

LIMERICK

Eamonn Scollard

Brian Begley   Diarmuid Sheehy   Ger O'Connor (Captain)

Jason Stokes   Tom McGarry   Martin Dineen

John Galvin   John Quane

Fergal Finnan   Pat Ahern   Michael O'Doherty

Michael Reidy   Noel Mulvihill   Colm Hickey

SUBSTITUTES: Eddie Scully for Fergal Finnan; Derek Ryan for Noel Mulvihill;
Noel Frewen for Eddie Scully

CORK
BACK ROW L TO R: Nicholas Murphy, Alan O'Regan, Damien O'Neill, Ronan McCarthy, Micheál O'Sullivan,
Ciarán O'Sullivan, Joe Kavanagh, Seán Óg Ó hAilpín, Mark O'Sullivan
FRONT ROW L TO Podsie O'Mahony, Martin Cronin, Kevin O'Dwyer, Eoin Sexton, Anthony Lynch, Aidan Dorgan

LIMERCIK
BACK ROW L TO R: Fergal Finnan, John Galvin, Brian Begley, John Quane, Martin Dineen, Tom McGarry, Diarmuid Sheehy, Jason Stokes, Eamonn Scollard
FRONT ROW L TO R: Michael Reidy, Pat Ahern, Ger O'Connor, Colm Hickey, Noel Mulvihill, Michael O'Doherty

SUNDAY, JUNE 20, 1999

MUNSTER SENIOR FOOTBALL CHAMPIONSHIP SEMI-FINAL

KERRY versus CLARE

FITZGERALD STADIUM (KILLARNEY)

REFEREE: MICHAEL CURLEY (GALWAY)

RESULT: KERRY 3-17 CLARE 0-12

CONFIDENT KERRY PRODUCED ONE of their best displays for some considerable time when they completely overwhelmed an injury-stricken Clare team to set up a Munster Final clash with old-rivals Cork. This was Kerry football at its brilliant best and Clare were simply unable to cope with the sheer power, pace and clinical finishing of the defending champions who scored no less than 3-11 from play. But Kerry's performance must be measured against the level of opposition provided by a Clare side missing injured players Ger Keane, Joe Considine, Donal O'Sullivan, Frankie Griffin, Michael Hynes and Alan Malone. Clare could ill-afford to be without such influential players against a Kerry team in such devastating form as witnessed in this one-sided Munster semi-final. Odhran O'Dwyer and Ciaran Considine were also struggling with injury but came on as substitutes in the course of the second half in an attempt to retrieve an almost impossible situation.

Clare, favoured by the breeze, recovered well from a superb goal by Kerry captain John Crowley in the 8th minute with two good points from Peadar McMahon and Mark O'Connell. But there was little for Clare to enthuse about after Dara Ó Cinnéide scored Kerry's second goal in the 20th minute, following good approach work by Dara Ó Sé and Noel Kennelly, who supplied the final pass. The under-pressure Clare defence was caught out once more in the 26th minute when John Crowley scored his second goal. Dara Ó Cinnéide, Aodán MacGearailt and John McGlynn were involved in the build-up before the in-form Crowley, returning to the side after a lengthy absence through injury, despatched the ball past James Hanrahan for another spectacular goal to leave Kerry 3-5 to 0-5 in front by the 26th minute. Denis Russell scored his second point from a free before the finish of the opening half as Clare continued to battle against overwhelming odds. Kerry's direct play reaped dividends and the three goals could be filed under the 'top-drawer' category.

Kerry were comfortably ahead, 3-6 to 0-7, at half-time and a point each from Maurice Fitzgerald and Aodán MacGearailt increased their lead early in the second half. At this juncture, it was clear for all to see that a spirited Clare team had little chance of recovering lost ground. Kerry were dominant in nearly every sector of the field and with Maurice Fitzgerald in flying form there could only be one result. His sixth point in the 56th minute pushed Kerry 3-13 to 0-10 clear. But it would be unfair to single out Maurice Fitzgerald as every Kerry forward was a danger man and all six found the target in a superlative display of score taking.

One had to feel sympathy for the Clare players and their dedicated manager, Tommy Curtin, who saw all his hard work come to naught because of an injury crisis that would have adversely affected any team in the land. To their credit, Clare played plenty of positive football outfield with Denis Russell prominent at midfield but their defence found the flying Kerry forwards too hot to handle. It was as simple as that! Kerry forwards held the key and they unlocked the Banner defence time and again with some precision passing and expertly taken scores.

Eamonn Breen scored the last point of the game to leave the large contingent of Kerry supporters' in a happy mood, contemplating a Munster Final showdown with Cork. Rest assured, an entirely different proposition, altogether!

SCORERS - KERRY: Maurice Fitzgerald 0-6; John Crowley 2-0; Aodán MacGearailt 0-4; Dara Ó Cinnéide 1-1; John McGlynn 0-3; Dara Ó Sé 0-1; Noel Kennelly 0-1; Eamonn Breen 0-1
CLARE: Denis Russell 0-3; Peadar McMahon 0-2; Colm Mullen 0-2; Brian McMahon 0-2; Mark O'Connell 0-1; Odhran O'Dwyer 0-1; Ciaran Considine 0-1

KERRY

Declan O'Keeffe

Michael McCarthy Barry O'Shea Killian Burns

Tomás Ó Sé Seamus Moynihan Eamonn Breen

Dara Ó Sé Donal Daly

John McGlynn Noel Kennelly Dara Ó Cinnéide

John Crowley (Captain) Aodán MacGearailt Maurice Fitzgerald

SUBSTITUTES: Billy O'Shea for Maurice Fitzgerald; William Kirby for Dara Ó Sé;
Mike Hassett for Tomás Ó Sé

CLARE

James Hanrahan

Conor Whelan Niall Hawes John Enright

Padraig Gallagher Brian Considine Barry Keating

Denis Russell Brendan Rouine (Captain)

Mark O'Connell Peadar McMahon Denis O'Driscoll

Colm Mullen Brian McMahon Martin Daly

SUBSTITUTES: Cathal Nagle for John Enright; Odhran O'Dwyer for Denis O'Driscoll;
Ciaran Considine for Martin Daly

KERRY
BACK ROW L TO R: Dara Ó Sé, Barry O'Shea, Noel Kennelly, John McGlynn, Donal Daly, Maurice Fitzgerald,
Aodán Mac Gearailt
FRONT ROW L TO R: Dara Ó Cinnéide, Tomás Ó Sé, Killian Burns, Declan O'Keeffe, John Crowley, Seamus Moynihan,
Michael McCarthy, Eamonn Breen

CLARE
BACK ROW L TO R: Peadar McMahon, Niall Hawes, Brian Considine, Martin Daly, James Hanrahan, Conor Whelan, Brian McMahon, Denis Russell
FRONT ROW L TO R: Denis O'Driscoll, Barry Keating, Colm Mullen, Brendan Rouine, Mark O'Connell, John Enright, Padraig Gallagher

SUNDAY, JULY 18, 1999

MUNSTER SENIOR FOOTBALL CHAMPIONSHIP FINAL

CORK versus KERRY

PÁIRC UÍ CHAOIMH

REFEREE: PAT MC ENEANEY (MONAGHAN)

RESULT: CORK 2-10 KERRY 2-4

THE EMOTION IN LARRY TOMPKINS' VOICE immediately after the game clearly demonstrated in a very tangible way what this victory meant to everyone involved with this Cork team. Proud manager, Tompkins, captain of the Cork team that won the All-Ireland title in 1990, was grinning from ear to ear as jubilant supporters celebrated with wild abandon. Tompkins was under pressure to deliver a winning performance and his team duly obliged in a game that Cork thoroughly deserved to win to complete the Munster Football and Hurling double. Fiji born, Seán Óg Ó hAilpín, a member of both teams, best epitomised Cork's character and resilience. Ó hAilpín had an uneasy first-half during which Aodán MacGearailt scored two goals but the dual star showed commendable courage to produce an excellent second half display as his colleagues in the Cork defence, Ronan McCarthy, Anthony Lynch, Ciarán O'Sullivan, Eoin Sexton and Martin Cronin all played superbly. Micheál O'Sullivan was the dominant player at midfield with a performance of real quality that paved the way for Cork's memorable victory. Don Davis was simply superb throughout and proved his undoubted ability while substitutes Fachtna Collins and Fionán Murray scored the vital goals. Philip Clifford and Podsie O'Mahony accounted for four points each as Cork outscored Kerry by 2-5 to 0-2 in a stunning second half display to claim their 32nd Provincial title.

Incredibly, Kerry's brilliant star, Maurice Fitzgerald, one of the most outstanding players the game has ever seen, failed to land a single score in the course of the game. Fitzgerald, '1997 Footballer of the Year', was desperately unlucky not to score a goal after just twenty seconds play when his shot skimmed narrowly wide of the post. It was a let off for Cork. Fitzgerald's artistry was in evidence in Kerry's opening goal in the 17th minute when he somehow delivered a pass to Donal Daly. MacGearailt gathered Daly's effort and scored a superb goal. The Gaeltacht marksman scored another splendid goal in the 33rd minute to give Kerry a three points advantage, 2-2 to 0-5, at half-time. Those two goals disguised weaknesses in the Kerry make up and those deficiencies became increasingly more evident as the game wore on and Cork began to exert their influence. Philip Clifford scored three points for Cork in the first half while Joe Kavanagh and Podsie O'Mahony got the other scores. John Crowley and John McGlynn scored a point each for Kerry but MacGearailt's goals were the main highlights of a stop-start, dour first half where there were a number of flare-ups and off the ball incidents. Corner back Michael McCarthy was outstanding for Kerry in the first half with Seamus Moynihan also very prominent. Indeed, Moynihan continued to play superbly as Kerry fought gallantly to keep their Championship hopes alive. The Kerry half forwards made little impact in the second half as Ciarán O'Sullivan, Eoin Sexton and the very impressive Martin Cronin played superbly in the Cork defence.

Cork had drawn level by the 13th minute of the second half through points from Micheál O'Sullivan, Podsie O'Mahony and a splendid effort from Philip Clifford. Cork were now dominant in most areas and took a giant step towards reclaiming the Munster title when substitute Fachtna Collins scored an opportunist goal after Declan O'Keeffe failed to hold a high ball. John Crowley replied with a point for Kerry in the 55th minute – their first score of the second half – and substitute William Kirby then closed the gap to the minimum with a fine point. But Kerry's hopes of retaining their title were well and truly dashed in the 62nd minute when Mark O'Sullivan broke the ball down to Fionán Murray who scored the decisive goal.

Typically, Kerry fought the good fight to the very finish but the Cork defence stood firm. Anthony Lynch blocked a goal effort from John Crowley while Seán Óg Ó hAilpín bravely denied substitute Billy O'Shea a goal late in the game.

Thousands of Cork supporters raced on to the field to congratulate their heroes after the game for their magnificent victory over their arch-rivals, as Larry Tompkins paid tribute to everyone involved with the team for their hard-work and commitment.

SCORERS – CORK: Philip Clifford 0-4; Podsie O'Mahony 0-4; Fachtna Collins 1-0;
Fionán Murray 1-0; Joe Kavanagh 0-1; Micheál O'Sullivan 0-1;
KERRY: Aodán MacGearailt 2-0; John Crowley 0-2; John McGlynn 0-1; William Kirby 0-1

CORK

Kevin O'Dwyer

Ronan McCarthy   Seán Óg Ó hAilpín   Anthony Lynch

Ciarán O'Sullivan   Eoin Sexton   Martin Cronin

Nicholas Murphy   Micheál O'Sullivan

Brendan Jer O'Sullivan   Joe Kavanagh   Podsie O'Mahony

Philip Clifford (Captain)   Don Davis   Mark O'Sullivan

SUBSTITUTES: Fachtna Collins for Brendan Jer O'Sullivan;
Fionán Murray for Nicholas Murphy

KERRY

Declan O'Keeffe

Michael McCarthy   Barry O'Shea   Killian Burns

Tomás Ó Sé   Seamus Moynihan   Eamonn Breen

Dara Ó Sé   Donal Daly

John McGlynn   Liam Hassett   Dara Ó Cinnéide

John Crowley (Captain)   Aodán MacGearailt   Maurice Fitzgerald

SUBSTITUTES: Billy O'Shea for Liam Hassett; William Kirby for John McGlynn;
Mike Frank Russell for Aodán MacGearailt

CORK
BACK ROW L TO R: Alan Quirke, Alan O'Regan, John Miskella, Martin Cronin, Joe Kavanagh, Nicholas Murphy,
Micheál O'Sullivan, Mark O'Sullivan, Ronan McCarthy, Seán Óg Ó hAilpín, Micheál Cronin, Don Davis
FRONT ROW L TO R: Mark O'Connor, Brendan Walsh, Fionán Murray, Podsie O'Mahony, Ciarán O'Sullivan, Eoin Sexton,
Philip Clifford, Kevin O'Dwyer, Brendan Jer O'Sullivan, Anthony Lynch, Fachtna Collins

KERRY
BACK ROW L TO R: Dara Ó Sé, Barry O'Shea, Liam Hassett, John McGlynn, Donal Daly, Michael McCarthy, Aodán Mac Gearailt, Tomás Ó Sé
FRONT ROW L TO R: Seamus Moynihan, John Crowley, Declan O'Keeffe, Dara Ó Cinneíde, Killian Burns, Eamonn Breen, Maurice Fitzgerald

SATURDAY, MAY 29, 1999

CONNACHT SENIOR FOOTBALL CHAMPIONSHIP

MAYO versus NEW YORK

McHALE PARK (CASTLEBAR)

REFEREE: SEAMUS PRIOR (LEITRIM)

RESULT: MAYO 3-13 NEW YORK 0-10

NO ONE REALISTICALLY EXPECTED NEW YORK to present too many problems for Mayo and as it turned out there was never any likelihood of an upset at McHale Park. New York, appearing in the Championship for the very first time, suffered a huge setback when key defenders Donal Breslin and Owen Cummins were forced to withdraw from the team because of injury. Full-forward Brian McCabe moved to centre-half-back in place of Cummins while left-half-forward Jim Donohue switched to right-half-back to replace Breslin. Those enforced positional changes totally disrupted the New York defence and severely restricted their options in a considerably weakened forward division.

Although Mayo had too much guile, experience and football know-how for the visitors, there were many positive aspects to New York's play with Michael Slowey, Pat Mahoney, William O'Donnell and Neville Dunne all performing admirably in the face of tremendous pressure. Despite their twelve-point winning margin, Mayo shot ten wides in the first half, and improvement will be required in that area. Midfielder William O'Donnell landed New York's first ever point in the Championship in the 18th minute by which stage, Mayo had 1-4 on the scoreboard.

David Nestor brilliantly rounded corner-back Gerry Kelly to drive the ball past New York goalkeeper Chicago-born Emmet Haughian for Mayo's opening goal which arrived after less than five minutes play. Nestor whipped over a point from the left wing in the 7th minute as Mayo established a firm grip on the game. James Horan, Maurice Sheridan and Colm McManamon added a point each to leave Mayo 1-4 to 0-0 ahead midway through the first half. New York's grit and determination began to pay dividends when O'Donnell, Pat Mahoney and Stephen Cassidy scored a point each. The visitors were dealt a severe body blow at the end of the first half when Colm McManamon finished the ball to the net after a pass from Nestor, which left Mayo 2-6 to 0-3 in front at half-time.

New York rallied briefly on the resumption and scored two quick points in a four minute period from Michael Slowey and William O'Donnell, but with Nestor, Horan and McManamon in good scoring form, Mayo had moved 2-10 to 0-7 ahead by the 47th minute.

Pat Mahoney and Michael Slowey fired over a point each – both superb efforts – before Mayo again took complete control and substitute Brian Maloney scored an excellent goal.

It was a brave performance by New York against a far stronger and mobile Mayo side that at times moved with great fluency but on other occasions appeared to revert back to their old habits. A better equipped team than New York would have made them pay dearly for defensive errors and wayward marksmanship. On the other hand, the in-form Horan, MacManamon, Sheridan and Nestor all took some great scores while Kevin Cahill and David Heaney along with championship debutantes Gordon Morley and Aidan Higgins played well in defence. Liam McHale made an impact at midfield when he replaced the injured David Brady late in the first half and looks a player that still has something to offer Mayo football. The Mayo players are still as keen as ever and it would be unwise for anyone to discount John Maughan's team in 'Championship '99.

SCORERS – MAYO: Colm McManamon 1-3; Maurice Sheridan 0-5; David Nestor 1-2;
James Horan 0-3; Brian Maloney 1-0
NEW YORK: Michael Slowey 0-3; Pat Mahoney 0-2; William O'Donnell 0-2; Stephen Cassidy 0-1;
Edmond Cleary 0-1; Kieran Keaveney 0-1

MAYO

Peter Burke

Aidan Higgins   Kevin Cahill   Gordon Morley

Fergal Costello (Captain)   David Heaney   Noel Connelly

James Nallen   David Brady

Maurice Sheridan   James Horan   Colm McManamon

Michael Moyles   Ger Brady   David Nestor

SUBSTITUTES: Liam McHale for David Brady; Brian Maloney for Michael Moyles

NEW YORK

Emmet Haughian

Gerry Kelly   Seán Teague   Neville Dunne (Captain)

Jim Donohue   Brian McCabe   Richie Purcell

Pat Mahoney   Gary Dowd

William O'Donnell   Michael Slowey   Kieran Keaveney

Kevin Lilly   Stephen Cassidy   Eddie Murphy

SUBSTITUTES: Joe Cassidy for Gerry Kelly; Edmond Cleary for Gary Dowd;
Enda Henry for Eddie Murphy

MAYO
BACK ROW L TO R: James Horan, Ger Brady, David Heaney, Michael Moyles, Peter Burke, David Brady, Maurice Sheridan, James Nallen, Kevin Cahill, Colm McManamon
FRONT ROW L TO R: Noel Connelly, Aidan Higgins, Fergal Costello, David Nestor, Gordon Morley

SUNDAY, MAY 30, 1999

CONNACHT SENIOR FOOTBALL CHAMPIONSHIP

ROSCOMMON versus LEITRIM

PÁIRC SEÁN MAC DIARMADA (CARRICK-ON-SHANNON)

REFEREE: BRENDAN GORMAN (ARMAGH)

RESULT: ROSCOMMON 0-15 LEITRIM 1-7

NOT EXACTLY AN AWE-INSPIRING DISPLAY by Roscommon but nevertheless more than sufficient on the day to see off the challenge of a plucky Leitrim side that firmly put behind them the shattering fourteen-points defeat by Galway in last year's Championship. Recently appointed Leitrim manager, Joe Reynolds, who took over the position from Peter McGinnity, had his young team remarkably well prepared considering his short time in charge. Leitrim produced a solid, workmanlike display, which belied their dismal League form, and an opportunist goal from wing-forward Christopher Carroll near the end of the opening half ensured the sides were on level terms at the interval. But Roscommon, inspired by substitute Fergal O'Donnell, pulled away after the re-start with four unanswered points that effectively ended Leitrim's championship hopes for yet another year.

Roscommon began confidently and had moved 0-4 to 0-1ahead by the 12th minute, with Eddie Lohan accounting for three of those scores – two from placed kicks plus an excellent effort from play. Stephen Lohan and Aiden Rooney had swapped points in the early exchanges. As the game settled to a pattern, it became apparent that the in-form Jason Ward and Paul McDermott had the edge at midfield over Roscommon pairing Tom Ryan and Stephen Lohan. Underdogs Leitrim won an abundance of possession in that midfield sector but the forwards spurned far too many scoring chances. The usually reliable Aiden Rooney had one of those off-days that every free-taker encounters from time to time. Goalkeeper Derek Thompson had a fine game for Roscommon and was quickly off his line to clear a through ball as Adrian Charles advanced with speed. Moments later, Thompson brilliantly saved an effort from defender Ciaran Murray following a splendid move involving Adrian Charles and Colin McGlynn.

The Leitrim goal eventually arrived just before half-time when Christopher Carroll shot to the net after latching on to a breaking ball from an Aiden Rooney free. Carroll's goal brought the sides level, Leitrim 1-3 Roscommon 0-6, at the interval.

O'Donnell's introduction at the start of the second half in place of Derek Duggan, who was suffering from a stomach bug, had an immediate impact. The big Roscommon Gaels man provided the vital link between the forwards and midfield and his strength on the ball and quality distribution caused major difficulties for the Leitrim defence. O'Donnell was in inspirational form. Roscommon hit the scoring trail shortly after the re-start with a point from the impressive Conor Connelly. Lorcan Dowd tacked on two more points from play and Frankie Dolan then scored a superb point to push Roscommon 0-10 to 1-3 ahead. That scoring spree put paid to any notions Leitrim had of causing an upset. Indeed the outcome was never in doubt once Roscommon began winning the vital breaks at midfield thanks to the contribution of O'Donnell.

Roscommon had increased their lead to six points by the 64th minute, just reward for some innovative and imaginative play. Frankie Dolan scored three fine points in the second half and had a huge influence on the game. Points from substitutes Fintan McBrien and Gene Bohan kept a spirited Leitrim side in touch but Roscommon substitute Nigel Dineen had the final say with a point from play to bring to an end a competitive and enjoyable encounter. As for Roscommon's future prospects, a huge improvement in all-round play will be required if the Mayo challenge is to be surmounted in Castlebar. Interestingly, Roscommon scored thirteen points from play, a quite remarkable achievement!

SCORERS – ROSCOMMON: Eddie Lohan 0-3; Frankie Dolan 0-3; Stephen Lohan 0-2; Conor Connelly 0-2; Lorcan Dowd 0-2; Nigel Dineen 0-2; Derek Duggan 0-1
LEITRIM: Christopher Carroll 1-1; Jason Ward 0-1; Aiden Rooney 0-1; Adrian Charles 0-1; Pat Farrell 0-1; Fintan McBrien 0-1; Gene Bohan 0-1

ROSCOMMON

Derek Thompson

| Denis Gavin | Damien Donlon | Enon Gavin |
| Rossa O'Callaghan | Clifford McDonald (Captain) | Ciaran Heneghan |

Tom Ryan Stephen Lohan

| Conor Connelly | Derek Duggan | Eddie Lohan |
| Frankie Dolan | Francie Grehan | Lorcan Dowd |

SUBSTITUTES: Fergus O'Donnell for Derek Duggan; Nigel Dineen for Francie Grehan; Michael Ryan for Ciaran Heneghan

---

LEITRIM

Gareth Phelan

| James Phelan | Seamus Quinn | Derek Kelleher |
| Seamus Dillon | Ciaran Murray | Padraig Flynn |

Paul McDermott Jason Ward

| Benny Guckian | Colin Regan | Christopher Carroll |
| Aiden Rooney | Colin McGlynn | Adrian Charles |

SUBSTITUTES: Pat Farell for Aiden Rooney; Fintan McBrien for Colin McGlynn; Gene Bohan for Benny Guckian

ROSCOMMON

BACK ROW L TO R: Eddie Lohan, Damien Donlon, Derek Thompson, Derek Duggan, Enon Gavin, Stephen Lohan, Conor Connelly

FRONT ROW L TO R: Francie Grehan, Denis Gavin, Tom Ryan, Clifford McDonald, Lorcan Dowd, Rossa O'Callaghan, Ciarán Heneghan, Frankie Dolan

LEITRIM

BACK ROW L TO R: Paul McDermott, Padraig Flynn, Jason Ward, Gareth Phelan, Christopher Carroll, Seamus Quinn, Ciaran Murray, Adrian Charles

FRONT ROW L TO R: James Phelan, Seamus Dillon, Aiden Rooney, Derek Kelleher, Benny Guckian, Colin Regan, Colin McGlynn

SUNDAY, JUNE 6, 1999
CONNACHT SENIOR FOOTBALL CHAMPIONSHIP

GALWAY versus LONDON

EMERALD PARK (RUISLIP)
REFEREE: EDDIE NEARY (SLIGO)
RESULT: GALWAY 1-18 LONDON 1-8

GALWAY CREATED HISTORY BY BECOMING the first county to begin the defence of their All-Ireland crown outside the country with a visit to Ruislip to take on London in the opening round of the Connacht Football Championship. It was a truly historic occasion and the sell-out crowd gave Galway a rousing reception worthy of their status as All-Ireland Champions. London produced a very positive and admirable display and caused more than a fair share of problems for a less than impressive Galway side, minus All-Ireland winning players Gary Fahy, Tomás Mannion, Kevin Walsh and Michael Donnellan. Fahy replaced John Divilly midway through the second half and from his customary full back position, helped steady Galway at a vital stage of the game, when London had closed the gap to just four points. Damien Mitchell was switched to centre-half-back to curb the threat of Terry McGivern. Galway coasted to a ten points half-time lead, 1-10 to 0-3, but a very capable London side, favoured by a strong breeze, rocked the champions by scoring 1-4 within fourteen minutes of the restart.

Julian Grimes scored the London goal in the 42nd minute, after a '45 by Tom Feehan came off the upright. Padraic Joyce replied with a point for Galway but London continued to surge forward in search of scores. High-fielding Jody Gormley landed a superb point and Terry McGivern proved his ability with two further points to bring his tally to three and cause plenty of nervousness among the Galway management and their large following.

Indeed, the Exiles were unlucky not to edge even closer as Tom Feehan had a goal disallowed and corner-forward Tommy Maguire hit the post after a good movement. Thereafter, Galway regained control and ran out comfortable winners on a 1-18 to 1-8 scoreline. The game once again demonstrated that Galway, as we already know, has a quality forward line and the return of Michael Donnellan for the Sligo clash will strengthen it still further.

Padraic Joyce scored 1-2 in the opening eight minutes and it became bleaker still for London when Niall Finnegan sent over a free and Jaralath Fallon fisted a point. It could have been worse for London had corner back Barry McDonagh not blocked a Niall Finnegan shot on goal.

It took London nearly seventeen minutes to register their first score, which arrived courtesy of a point from play by Julian Grimes, the first ever score by the exiles against reigning All-Ireland Champions.

Terry McGivern and Derek Savage swapped points before Tommy Joyce kicked a magnificent sideline ball over the bar as Galway powered ahead.

Jarlath Fallon, with another fisted effort, along with Padraic Joyce and Paul Clancy, who became the sixth Galway forward to score, all scored a point each to push the visitors 1-9 to 0-2 ahead by the 30th minute of the first half. Midfielder Tony Murphy replied with a point for London but Jarlath Fallon closed the first half scoring with a point from play off his right foot. Fallon is a class player and appears to be holding the form that earned him the accolade, 'All-Star Footballer of the Year' in '98.

London's revival after the re-start exposed deficiencies in a Galway side that looked weary at stages, but at other times displayed some of the sharpness that brought them so much glory in '98.

After London's early second half surge, Galway regained the initiative with a point each from Seán Óg de Paor, Derek Savage, Niall Finnegan and Jarlath Fallon to leave Galway 1-15 to 1-7 in front.

A well-prepared London side continued to work hard in search of scores but found the Galway half-back line in defiant mood. Savage landed his third point and Finnegan scored two from play as Galway finished in the style of champions, but only after enduring a few anxious moments from a brave London side.

Substitute Paul Coggins scored the final point of the game for a brave London side that caused more than a few anxious moments for the visitors during the second half, but were unable to cope with the scoring power of the All-Ireland Champions in the closing stages.

SCORERS – GALWAY: Padraic Joyce 1-4; Niall Finnegan 0-4; Jarlath Fallon 0-4; Derek Savage 0-3; Tommy Joyce 0-1; Paul Clancy 0-1; Seán Óg de Paor 0-1
LONDON: Julian Grimes 1-1; Terry McGivern 0-3; Tommy Maguire 0-1; Tony Murphy 0-1; Jody Gormley 0-1; Paul Coggins 0-1

GALWAY		
	Martin McNamara	
Robin Doyle	Damien Mitchell	Tomás Meehan
Ray Silke (Captain)	John Divilly	Seán Óg de Paor
Seán Ó Domhnaill		Shay Walsh
Paul Clancy	Jarlath Fallon	Tommy Joyce
Derek Savage	Padraic Joyce	Niall Finnegan

SUBSTITUTES: Gary Fahy for John Divilly; Fergal Gavin for Shay Walsh; Declan Meehan for Tomás Meehan

LONDON

Dominic Kelly

Barry McDonagh	Pat Rafter	Finbar Downey
Conor Wilson	Dermot Gordon (Captain)	Brendan Bolger

Tony Murphy   Jody Gormley

Tom Feehan	Terry McGivern	Darragh Deering
Julian Grimes	Mick Galvin	Tommy Maguire

SUBSTITUTES: S O'Brien for Tony Murphy; Paul Coggins for Darragh Deering

GALWAY
BACK ROW L TO R: Padraic Joyce, Tomás Meehan, Shay Walsh, Seán Ó Domhnaill, Robin Doyle, Jarlath Fallon, John Divilly
FRONT ROW L TO R: Seán Óg de Paor, Damien Mitchell, Paul Clancy, Ray Silke, Derek Savage, Niall Finnegan, Tommy
Joyce, Martin McNamara

Féile na nGael

Enjoy Coca-Cola

REGISTERED TRADE MARK

suppo**RTE**rs

You don't have to be there to be there.

SUNDAY, JUNE 13, 1999

CONNACHT SENIOR FOOTBALL CHAMPIONSHIP SEMI-FINAL

MAYO versus ROSCOMMON

McHALE PARK (CASTLEBAR)

REFEREE: BRIAN WHITE (WEXFORD)

RESULT: MAYO 0-21 ROSCOMMON 0-10

MAYO FOOTBALLERS HAVE PRODUCED MANY outstanding performances since John Maughan took over as manager but few of those would compare to their second half display against a highly rated Roscommon side in this lopsided Connacht Football semi-final.

Mayo outscored Roscommon by 0-15 to 0-4 in a truly awesome second half display of point scoring that firmly laid to rest the view that the team was past its best. I said publicly before this game that Mayo are still a strong force, based on their experience and the number of quality players in their panel. And there are quite a few! What some people seemed to ignore in the build up to the game was that Mayo were unlucky not win two All-Ireland titles in the nineties and it was apparent before the Roscommon game that John Maughan had his team fresh and focussed for the task at hand. It is hard to know if Roscommon took their eye off the ball with a view to bigger days ahead, but the players learned the harsh realities of life against a razor sharp Mayo team that swept to victory with style and panache. Roscommon, so unlucky not to beat eventual All-Ireland Champions Galway in last year's Connacht Final, appeared disjointed and leaderless once Mayo began to forge ahead.

Roscommon had no answer to Mayo's support play, work rate and score taking in the second half as Maurice Sheridan, Colm McManamon, John Casey, James Horan, Noel Connelly and Kenneth Mortimer all found the target. Sheridan finished the game as top scorer with the very considerable contribution of nine points. Young Gordon Morley, a player of immense potential, turned in a superb display in a strong and resolute Mayo defence; James Nallen and David Brady played splendidly at midfield while the forwards ran riot in the second half. Mortimer played a key role in Mayo's victory in the second half as he distributed the ball with telling effect and created numerous chances for his forward colleagues. John Casey scored no fewer than six points from play in a 'Man of the Match' display. Roscommon played their best football in the opening half, during which the sides were level on no less than four occasions to underline the close nature of the exchanges. Roscommon full back Damien Donlon suffered an injury just before half-time and was unable to play any part in the game after the break. His absence represented a huge setback for Roscommon, who stumbled from one crisis to another throughout the course of a surprisingly one-sided second half.

The sides were tied 0-6 apiece at half-time and there was no indication whatsoever at that stage of what was about to unfold in the second half. There were many positive aspects to Roscommon's play in that opening half but many of their leading players were marked absent after the break much to the dismay of their large following. Any flaws evident in Mayo's game in the opening half disappeared without trace after the interval and it could have been worse for Roscommon had not Denis Gavin deflected a powerful Maurice Sheridan shot over the crossbar.

Fergal O'Donnell and Derek Duggan gave Roscommon an early advantage with a point each before Noel Connelly landed an excellent point from play in the 8th minute to open Mayo's account. Duggan increased Roscommon's lead with a point from play before in-form duo John Casey and Maurice Sheridan sent over a point each to level the match for the first time. Both sides enjoyed spells of dominance and the sides were level on three further occasions before referee Brian White called a halt to what was an entertaining if not exactly awe-inspiring first half. Casey scored two points in the second quarter while the hard-working Francie Grehan did likewise for Roscommon.

Favoured by the breeze, an inspired Mayo side availed of every opportunity to display their undoubted talents after the interval and two points from Maurice Sheridan set the trend for the remainder of the game. Mayo hit over a flurry of points from all angles as shell-shocked Roscommon floundered. Mayo played some exhibition football in the course of the second half to underline their superiority and give notice of their intentions in 'Championship '99'.

Roscommon's inexplicable second half collapse will cause concern, not only for manager Gay Sheeran, but for every follower of the game within the county. But it is not all doom and gloom. There are many outstanding players on the panel and in Gay Sheeran, Roscommon have a first-rate manager, who will no doubt analyse what went wrong against Mayo and set about rectifying the problem for the future.

SCORERS – MAYO: Maurice Sheridan 0-9; John Casey 0-6; Noel Connelly 0-2; Colm McManamon 0-2; James Horan 0-1; Kenneth Mortimer 0-1
ROSCOMMON: Derek Duggan 0-4; Fergal O'Donnell 0-3; Francie Grehan 0-2; Frankie Dolan 0-1

MAYO

Peter Burke

Aidan Higgins   Kevin Cahill   Gordon Morley
Fergal Costello   David Heaney   Noel Connelly

James Nallen   David Brady

Colm McManamon   Kenneth Mortimer (Captain)   John Casey
Maurice Sheridan   James Horan   David Nestor

SUBSTITUTES: Ger Brady for David Nestor; Pat Fallon for James Nallen;
Brian Ruane for Noel Connelly

ROSCOMMON

Derek Thompson

Denis Gavin   Damien Donlon   Enon Gavin

Rossa O'Callaghan   Clifford McDonald (Captain)   Ciaran Heneghan

Tom Ryan   Stephen Lohan

Conor Connelly   Fergal O'Donnell   Derek Duggan

Frankie Dolan   Francie Grehan   Lorcan Dowd

SUBSTITUTES: Michael Ryan for Damien Donlon; Nigel Dineen for Francie Grehan;
Ger Keane for Stephen Lohan

MAYO
BACK ROW L TO R: David Nestor, James Horan, John Casey, Peter Burke, David Brady, David Heaney, James Nallen, Kevin Cahill, Maurice Sheridan
FRONT ROW L TO R: Fergal Costello, Colm McManamon, Aidan Higgins, Kenneth Mortimer, Noel Connelly, Gordon Morley

ROSCOMMON
BACK ROW L TO R: Fergal O'Donnell, Denis Gavin, Enon Gavin, Derek Thompson, Derek Duggan, Damien Donlon, Stephen Lohan, Conor Connelly
FRONT ROW L TO R: Ciaran Heneghan, Lorcan Dowd, Tom Ryan, Clifford McDonald, Rossa O'Callaghan, Frankie Dolan, Francie Grehan

SUNDAY, JUNE 27, 1999

CONNACHT SENIOR FOOTBALL CHAMPIONSHIP SEMI-FINAL

GALWAY versus SLIGO

MARKIEVICZ PARK (SLIGO)

REFEREE: PADDY RUSSELL (TIPPERARY)

RESULT: GALWAY 1-13 SLIGO 3-7 (A DRAW)

IT WAS AS DRAMATIC A FINISH to a Connacht Championship game as ever witnessed at the famed Markeivicz Park venue in Sligo. Galway came to the picturesque ground as All-Ireland Champions and were extremely fortunate not to relinquish their crown to a courageous and well-organised Sligo side. The noise reached a crescendo when Brian Walsh fisted a high ball from Paul Durcan to the net for his second goal with less than two minutes remaining to push Sligo ahead for only the second time in the game. Galway supporters looked on in disbelief at events unfolding before their eyes as the large Sligo following celebrated with wild abandon. But Galway proved their pedigree with a late surge, which yielded a close-in free after Paul Clancy was fouled. Ice-cool Padraic Joyce sent over the levelling point from a free to force a replay a week later at Tuam Stadium. From the kick-out, referee Paddy Russell blew the full-time whistle to signal the end to a game in which Galway had played well-below par and came perilously close to bowing out of the Championship. Yet, the All-Ireland Champions, despite some evident weaknesses, were slightly the more accomplished side all through and their forward line, minus Jarlath Fallon and Niall Finnegan, caused many anxious moments for a less than assured Sligo back line. The Galway defence was very susceptible to the high ball throughout the game and 1998 All-Star goalkeeper, Martin McNamara had an uncomfortable afternoon. Sligo midfielder Eamonn O'Hara told me afterwards that his team were struggling throughout and did not play to their set plan. "We were changing tactics during the game but we got a late goal and thought we had won the game. I suppose Sligo people will say it was a dubious free kick that levelled the match while Galway will say it was a deserved free. I think a draw was a fair result overall, but it was disappointing at the end not to win. We didn't play up to our potential but fair play also to Galway for showing their grit and determination to come back and get the draw."

Seán Ó Domhnaill was very relieved to see Padraic Joyce send over the equalising point. The giant Galway midfielder admitted his heart sank when Brian Walsh scored his second goal to put Sligo in front. "It flashed through my mind that it could be the end of us, but fair play to Martin McNamara for kicking the ball out to Fergal Gavin who gave it to Paul Clancy and he won the free. The pressure was on Padraic Joyce to throw it over and he did. That's what football is all about and it's now back to Tuam Stadium for the replay."

After a bright opening, during which Eamonn O'Hara and Ken Killeen, raced through a hesitant Galway defence to score a point each, Sligo let the initiative slip and the old flaws began to surface.

Instead of getting the ball quickly into their forward line, Sligo reverted back to short passing, held up the ball too long and the more experienced Galway side took advantage. Paul Clancy opened the scoring for Galway in the 7th minute and then John Donnellan sent over the equalising point.

Padraic Joyce converted a free and Paul Clancy scored his second point to leave Galway 0-4 to 0-2 ahead by the 27th minute. Paul Taylor replied with a pointed free for Sligo but Galway finished the first half in impressive fashion scoring 1-2 in a blistering three-minute spell. Firstly, Seán Óg de Paor moved upfield to kick a splendid point; John Donnellan then scored his second point of the game while Derek Savage put some daylight between the teams with a fine goal to leave Galway 1-6 to 0-3 ahead at half-time. When midfielder Kevin Walsh increased Galway's lead with a point two minutes after the re-start, one felt the All-Ireland Champions were about to surge clear. But we seriously misjudged the character and resilience of the Sligo team. Brian Walsh scored a goal, following a mistake by Galway goalkeeper Martin McNamara, to give Sligo renewed hope. The highly energetic Paul Durcan, who produced an outstanding display at midfield, scored Sligo's second goal in the 45th minute to close the gap to the minimum. It was an anxious time for Galway!

Jarlath Fallon, who failed to start because of injury, proved a steadying influence when introduced in place of Shay Walsh in the Galway forward line. Paul Clancy and the impressive Padraic Joyce sent over a point each to leave the All-Ireland Champions 1-10 to 2-4 ahead by the 49th minute. Sligo, favoured by the breeze, won an abundance of possession in the closing quarter as they continued to press forward in search of scores. It was clear that Galway were now struggling to survive. It was tight, tense and exciting in those closing stages: Paul Taylor converted a free; then Brian Walsh scored his second goal to put Sligo in front before Padraic Joyce forced a replay with a late pointed free.

The All-Ireland Champions had escaped but only just! Next stop, Tuam Stadium, for the replay!

SCORERS – GALWAY: Padraic Joyce 0-4; Paul Clancy 0-3; Derek Savage 1-0; John Donnellan 0-2; Michael Donnellan 0-2; Seán Óg de Paor 0-1; Kevin Walsh 0-1
SLIGO: Brian Walsh 2-0; Paul Durcan 1-1; Eamonn O'Hara 0-2; Paul Taylor 0-2; Ken Killeen 0-2

GALWAY

Martin McNamara

Tomás Meehan	Gary Fahy	Tomás Mannion
Ray Silke (Captain)	John Divilly	Seán Óg de Paor

Kevin Walsh   Seán Ó Domhnaill

Paul Clancy	Shay Walsh	Michael Donnellan
Derek Savage	Padraic Joyce	John Donnellan

SUBSTITUTES: Jarlath Fallon for Shay Walsh; Fergal Gavin for Kevin Walsh; Niall Finnegan for Paul Clancy

---

SLIGO

Peter Walsh

James Joyce	Colin White	Mark Cosgrove
Noel McGuire	Nigel Clancy	Ronan Keane

Paul Durcan   Eamonn O'Hara

Eamonn Cawley	Brian Walsh	Ken Killeen
Seán Flannery	Paul Taylor (Captain)	Gerry McGowan

SUBSTITUTES: John McPartland for Gerry McGowan; Con O'Meara for Eamonn Cawley; Dessie Sloyane for Seán Flannery

GALWAY
BACK ROW L TO R: Padraic Joyce, John Donnellan, Gary Fahy, Seán Ó Domhnaill, Kevin Walsh, Tomás Meehan, Jarlath Fallon, John Divilly
FRONT ROW L TO R: Seán Óg de Paor, Michael Donnellan, Martin McNamara, Ray Silke, Derek Savage, Paul Clancy, Tomás Mannion

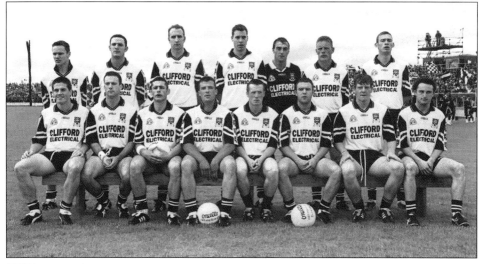

SLIGO
BACK ROW L TO R: Gerry McGowan, Brian Walsh, Paul Durcan, Nigel Clancy, Peter Walsh, Mark Cosgrove, Noel McGuire
FRONT ROW L TO R: Ronan Keane, Colin White, Eamonn O'Hara, Paul Taylor, Eamonn Cawley, Ken Killeen, Seán Flannery, James Joyce

SUNDAY, JULY 4, 1999

CONNACHT SENIOR FOOTBALL CHAMPIONSHIP SEMI-FINAL (REPLAY)

GALWAY versus SLIGO

TUAM STADIUM

REFEREE: PADDY RUSSELL (TIPPERARY)

RESULT: GALWAY 1-17 SLIGO 0-7

THIS GAME BORE NO RESEMBLANCE whatsoever to the drawn encounter at Markievicz Park a week earlier when Galway forward Padraic Joyce scored a late point to force a replay. This time round, the All-Ireland Champions romped home by thirteen points to set up a fascinating Connacht Final clash with Mayo. The general consensus in the build up to this replay was that Sligo had missed their chance and that Galway would make no mistake at the second time of asking. Pre-match predictions proved accurate, as Galway produced a display that was far superior to the one which saw them come within seconds of being dumped out of 'Championship '99' in the most dramatic of circumstances at Markievicz Park. Galway certainly encountered difficulties, particularly in the opening half, when a very determined Sligo team dominated for long stages, but the manner in which John O'Mahony's team pulled away after the break underlined the strength in depth of the All-Ireland Champions. It was easily Galway's best display since beating Kildare in last year's All-Ireland Final and no one should be in any doubt but that the men in maroon and white are still a formidable force.

Sligo missed a number of good scoring opportunities in the opening half and on the run of play deserved to be a few points ahead at half-time. Instead, the sides were level, 0-5 each at the interval, but like Roscommon in their semi-final against Mayo three weeks previously, Sligo were completely outclassed in the second half and could only score two points in reply to Galway's tally of 1-12.

John Donnellan, older brother of All-Star and '1998 Texaco Footballer of the Year', Michael, was Galway's star performer on the day. Donnellan never put a foot wrong and scored seven points – six from play – in what was a vintage display by the Dunmore man. John missed out on last year's glory trail but is now striking a rich vein of form, which can only be good news for the Champions. It was Donnellan who set the ball rolling after just one minute with a pointed free, but Sligo soon got into their stride and took a grip on the game. John McPartland, Paul Taylor and Dessie Sloyane fired over a point each to leave Sligo 0-3 to 0-1 ahead by the 10th minute. Galway found it extremely difficult to break down a resolute Sligo defence in the early stages as both sides endeavoured to gain the upperhand in what was a physical encounter between two very determined teams. Derek Savage scored a point from play for Galway in the 14th minute but with the breeze at their backs Sligo added to their tally with a point each from Dessie Sloyane and Ken Killeen to stretch their lead. Incredibly, Sligo could only score two points – both from placed kicks by Paul Taylor- for the remaining 50 minutes of the game as Galway lifted the pace and surged clear. But no one could fault Sligo midfielder Eamonn O'Hara who continued to battle for everything against overwhelming odds.

In the closing ten minutes of the first half, John Donnellan scored two points and Seán Óg de Paor kicked a trademark point to leave the sides level at the break. Galway, looking every inch the All-Ireland Champions, cut loose in the second half and Sligo, despite their best efforts, were helpless to stop the tidal wave of maroon and white. The Galway defence en bloc battened down the hatches; Kevin Walsh and Seán Ó Domhnaill gained the upperhand at midfield, although O'Hara never wilted, while the forwards picked off points with consummate ease. Walsh was a powerful force in the centre of the park and now appears to be back to his very best.

John Donnellan, Padraic Joyce from a '45 and Jarlath Fallon scored a point each within five minutes of the re-start and thereafter Galway took control with a display that bore all the hallmarks of a team returning to top form.

Paul Taylor converted a '45 after Martin McNamara blocked Dessie Sloyane's goal effort. By now Galway were in full flow and Derek Savage, John Donnellan and Seán Óg de Paor sent over a point apiece as their supporters roared approval. John Donnellan and Paul Taylor then exchanged points before Seán Óg de Paor rounded off a superb individual display with the only goal of the game. Galway scored 1-4 in the closing eight minutes of a game that had petered out as a contest long before that late flourish. Interestingly, John Donnellan scored the first and last point of the opening half and the first and last point of the second half.

SCORERS – GALWAY: John Donnellan 0-7; Seán Óg de Paor 1-2; Derek Savage 0-3; Jarlath Fallon 0-3; Padraic Joyce 0-1; Niall Finnegan 0-1
SLIGO: Paul Taylor 0-3; Dessie Sloyane 0-2; John McPartland 0-1; Ken Killeen 0-1

GALWAY

Martin McNamara

| Tomás Meehan | Gary Fahy | Tomás Mannion |
| Ray Silke (Captain) | John Divilly | Seán Óg de Paor |

Kevin Walsh   Seán Ó Domhnaill

| PPaul Clancy | Jarlath Fallon | Michael Donnellan |
| Derek Savage | Padraic Joyce | John Donnellan |

SUBSTITUTES: Niall Finnegan for Paul Clancy; Tommy Joyce for Michael Donnellan; Damien Mitchell for Gary Fahy

---

SLIGO

Peter Walsh

Noel McGuire	Colin White	Mark Cosgrove
James Joyce	Nigel Clancy	Ronan Keane

Paul Durcan   Eamonn O'Hara

Brian Walsh	Dessie Sloyane	Ken Killeen
John McPartland	Paul Taylor (Captain)	Seán Flannery

SUBSTITUTES: Con O'Meara for Seán Flannery; Brendan Kilcoyne for Mark Cosgrove; Philip Neary for John McPartland

GALWAY
BACK ROW L TO R: Padraic Joyce, John Donnellan, Seán Ó Domhnaill, Gary Fahy, Kevin Walsh, Jarlath Fallon, Tomás Mannion, John Divilly
FRONT ROW L TO R: Paul Clancy, Michael Donnellan, Martin McNamara, Ray Silke, Derek Savage, Seán Óg de Paor, Tomás Meehan

SLIGO
BACK ROW L TO R: James Joyce, Noel McGuire, Paul Durcan , Nigel Clancy, Peter Walsh, John McPartland, Mark Cosgrove, Colin White, Seán Flannery
FRONT ROW L TO R: Dessie Sloyane, Eamonn O'Hara, Paul Taylor, Ronan Keane, Brian Walsh, Ken Killeen

SUNDAY, JULY 18, 1999

CONNACHT SENIOR FOOTBALL CHAMPIONSHIP FINAL

GALWAY versus MAYO

TUAM STADIUM

REFEREE: BRIAN WHITE (WEXFORD)

RESULT: MAYO 1-14 GALWAY 1-10

THERE ARE FEW OCCASIONS IN IRISH SPORT to compare with the clash of Galway and Mayo in the Connacht Senior Football Championship Final as evidenced once again at Tuam Stadium in this riveting Provincial decider. It was a rain-sodden day in the North Galway town but the miserable conditions failed to dampen the enthusiasm of the 31,173 supporters who braved the elements to watch two totally committed and highly motivated teams. The presence of both the President of Ireland, Mary McAleese and the President of the G.A.A., Joe McDonagh, added to the sense of occasion, as the All-Ireland Champions put their title on the line on home territory. It was the first time reigning All-Ireland Champions had appeared in a Connacht Final for thirty-three years and supporters, only too well aware of the significance of the occasion, began to arrive in Tuam from early morning. There was a wonderful atmosphere in the ground by the time Wexford referee

Brian White started proceedings. Both teams were forced to make changes before the start of the game. Galway defender Gary Fahy had to withdraw because of a dead leg and Damien Mitchell from Menlough filled his place at full back. Mayo, too, had to line out without one of their key players. Former captain, Noel Connelly, failed a late fitness test on a hamstring injury, and Alan Roche from Davitt's was called into the team at left-half-back. As it turned out, Championship debutante Roche had an excellent game and more than justified his selection. John Divilly, who suffered slight injuries in a car accident on the Saturday before the game, took his place at centre half back for Galway and played quite well throughout. The first half represented everything positive in Gaelic Football as both sides enjoyed periods of dominance. There were seventeen scores in that opening half – fourteen from play, including two goals, while no fewer than five forwards from each side scored. Only Michael Donnellan and John Casey failed to find the target, although both players made solid contributions in general play in an action packed first half. Casey missed a glorious chance in the 52nd minute when he blazed wide in front of goal. Kieran McDonald later replaced Casey and scored the lead point in the 62nd minute.

Galway edged ahead with early points from Padraic Joyce and Derek Savage before James Horan settled Mayo with a point from play. It was a sign of things to come. Horan, born in Papakura, New Zealand, produced a superb display and his tally amounted to five points by match end. The teams were level, 0-5 apiece, by the 19th minute after good points from play for Galway by John Donnellan, Derek Savage and Niall Finnegan and equally impressive scores for Mayo from Kenneth Mortimer, David Nestor and James Horan.

Nestor scored the opening goal of the game in the 28th minute to put Mayo in front for the very first time in the game. Jarlath Fallon lost possession and the ball was kicked goalwards where it broke to Nestor who struck a rocket-like shot to the Galway net.

McMamamon scored his first point to stretch Mayo's lead but Galway hit back almost immediately. Mayo goalkeeper Peter Burke failed to hold a high centre from Seán Ó Domhnaill and Padraic Joyce kicked the ball to the net.

Galway finished the half with a flourish as Niall Finnegan, grandson of Seamus O'Malley who captained Mayo to a first All-Ireland senior success in 1936, and Jarlath Fallon scored a point each to leave the All-Ireland Champions 1-9 to 1-6 ahead at the interval.

John Donnellan increased Galway's lead within a minute of the re-start to push the All-Ireland Champions 1-10 to 1-6 ahead. Incredibly, Galway failed to score again for the remainder of the game.

As the match wore on, it became abundantly clear that the Mayo defence had the measure of the much vaunted Galway forward line that had frightened the daylights out of high-calibre defenders in 'Championship '98. David Heaney was outstanding at centre-half-back while around him players in green and red jerseys cleared their lines, tackled with ferocity, surged forward to link up with their midfield and forward colleagues and generally showed a hunger that Galway could not match on the day.

And yet, John O'Mahony's brave men, never gave up and only for a number of wides, six in the second half, could have been even closer at the finish. It should be remembered that Galway had a one point advantage with just fourteen minutes remaining, but at that stage the tide had begun to turn in favour of Mayo. The introduction of Kieran McDonald and Pat Fallon changed the course of the game. Fallon won some quality possession while McDonald caused panic in an already less than assured Galway back line. Horan's three points in a row levelled the game for only the second time in the 61st minute. McDonald and Fallon then scored a point each; Maurice Sheridan converted a '45 while James Nallen sealed a famous victory with a wonder point off his left foot to spark off massive celebrations among the Mayo faithful. Galway also had a let off in the closing stages when James Nallen was deprived of a goal when Tomás Meehan cleared the ball off the line. In 1997, Mayo defeated Galway at Tuam Stadium in a Championship game for the first time in 46 years and John Maughan's team are still a formidable force. Proud Galway, wonderful ambassadors as All-Ireland Champions, looked weary in the third quarter and eventually succumbed to a first-rate Mayo side that will certainly make a strong bid for All-Ireland honours.

SCORERS – MAYO: James Horan 0-5; David Nestor 1-1; Maurice Sheridan 0-3; Kenneth Mortimer 0-1; Colm McManamon 0-1; Pat Fallon 0-1; Kieran McDonald 0-1; James Nallen 0-1
GALWAY: Padraic Joyce 1-2; Niall Finnegan 0-3; John Donnellan 0-2; Derek Savage 0-2; Jarlath Fallon 0-1;

MAYO

Peter Burke

| Aidan Higgins | Kevin Cahill | Gordon Morley |
| Fergal Costello | David Heaney | Alan Roche |

James Nallen   David Brady

| Colm McManamon | James Horan | Kenneth Mortimer (Captain) |
| Maurice Sheridan | John Casey | David Nestor |

SUBSTITUTES: Pat Fallon for Colm McManamon; Kieran McDonald for John Casey

---

GALWAY

Martin McNamara

| Tomás Meehan | Damien Mitchell | Tomás Mannion |
| Ray Silke (Captain) | John Divilly | Seán Óg de Paor |

Kevin Walsh   Seán Ó Domhnaill

| Michael Donnellan | Jarlath Fallon | Niall Finnegan |
| Derek Savage | Padraic Joyce | John Donnellan |

SUBSTITUTE: Paul Clancy for John Donnellan

MAYO
BACK ROW L TO R: Kevin Cahill, David Heaney, John Casey, Peter Burke. David Brady, James Nallen, Maurice Sheridan, James Horan
FRONT ROW L TO R: David Nestor, Fergal Costello, Kenneth Mortimer, Aidan Higgins, Colm McManamon, Alan Roche, Gordon Morley

GALWAY
BACK ROW L TO R: Padraic Joyce, Damien Mitchell, John Donnellan, Seán Ó Domhnaill, Kevin Walsh, Tomás Meehan, Jarlath Fallon, John Divilly
FRONT ROW L TO R: Seán Óg de Paor, Michael Donnellan, Martin McNamara, Ray Silke, Derek Savage, Niall Finnegan, Tomás Mannion

Too young to play...

... but not too young to dream.
He may be little, but he has
his dreams. It's good to know
that when he's old enough to
play, **Cumann na mBunscol**
will be there to nurture and
guide him, so that one day he
may achieve his dream to play
in the **Church & General
National Leagues.**

By supporting Cumann na
mBunscol and the National
Leagues, Church & General
are helping to make his and
all our dreams come true.

Church & General
A company of the Allianz Group

SUNDAY, MAY 30, 1999

ULSTER SENIOR FOOTBALL CHAMPIONSHIP PRELIMINARY ROUND

MONAGHAN versus FERMANAGH

ST. TIGHEARNACH'S PARK (CLONES)

REFEREE: MICHAEL CONVERY (DERRY)

RESULT: FERMANAGH 2-12 MONAGHAN 1-10

THERE WAS JUBILATION AMONG FERMANAGH supporters as their footballers recorded their first success in the Ulster senior Championship for seven years with a five-point win over near neighbours Monaghan at St. Tighearnach's Park. This was a well-merited victory by a Fermanagh side that recovered their composure after a shaky start to produce some top class football that clearly underlined their rate of improvement in recent years. Fermanagh, whose last Championship victory was against Antrim in 1992, now meet Tyrone in the Ulster semi-final on the last Sunday in June.

The chances of a Fermanagh victory looked slim in the opening quarter during which Monaghan raced into a 1-4 to 0-2 lead with Declan Smyth from the Carrickmacross club scoring 1-2. Smyth opened the scoring with a goal from a penalty inside two minutes to give his side a dream start. Tom Brewster replied with a point from play for Fermanagh before Ian Larmer sent over a free to push Monaghan 1-1 to 0-1 ahead by the 7th minute. Shane King and Frank McEneaney swapped points before the in-form Smyth whipped over two points from play. Apart from Smyth, Darren Swift was causing more than a share of difficulties at this stage for an under-pressure Fermanagh back line while Noel Marron was highly effective in the Monaghan defence.

But to their credit, Fermanagh battled back courageously and with Tom Brewster in superb form, had moved one point clear by the half-time break. Shane King converted a penalty ten minutes before half-time after Dermot McDermott picked the ball off the ground. King's goal proved a major confidence booster and when the same player finished the ball to the net very early in the second half, after Monaghan goalkeeper Glen Murphy failed to hold a high ball from Seán Quinn, Fermanagh sensed it was going to be their day. Once the Fermanagh defence came to terms, without ever fully nullifying the obvious threat of Smyth, Monaghan's scores from play all but dried up. Monaghan could only muster a single pointed free from Ian Larmer, between the 14th and 41st minute which was a tribute to the great defensive work of Fermanagh, coupled with the midfield dominance of Paul Brewster and Liam McBarron, Monaghan continued to press forward in search of scores and their perseverance was rewarded with a point each from play from Peter Duffy, Smyth and substitute John Paul Mone, which reduced the deficit to just three points. Fermanagh came under increasing pressure and goalkeeper Cormac McAdam did will to deny Smyth a goal with a fine save. Smyth pointed a free in the 60th minute but Darren Swift was somewhat unlucky that his fisted effort was wide of the mark. The impressive Tom Brewster responded to the challenge with two splendid points from play while King had the final say with a point from a free. It was only Fermanagh's ninth Championship win in nearly forty years. The joy among their supporters as they painted Clones green and white, underlined what this victory meant to the people of Fermanagh after so many years of heartbreak and disappointment.

SCORERS – FERMANAGH: Shane King 2-2; Tom Brewster 0-6; Raymond Gallagher 0-2; Liam McBarron 0-1; Raymond Johnson 0-1
MONAGHAN: Declan Smyth 1-5; Ian Larmer 0-2; Peter Duffy 0-1; Frank McEneaney 0-1; John Paul Mone 0-1

FERMANAGH

Cormac McAdam

Tommy Callaghan   Paddy McGuinness (Captain)   Michael Lilly

Shaun Burns   Tony Collins   Kieran Gallagher

Paul Brewster   Liam McBarron

Raymond Johnson   Tom Brewster   Dara McGrath

Raymond Gallagher   Seán Quinn   Shane King

SUBSTITUTES: Shane McDermott for Dara McGrath; Colm Bradley for Tony Collins

---

MONAGHAN

Glen Murphy

Padraig McKenna   Dermot McDermott   Noel Marron

Edwin Murphy   Gerard McGuirk   John Conlon

Joe Coyle   Frank McEneaney

Darren Swift   Damien Freeman   Peter Duffy

Declan Smyth   Stephen McGinnity   Ian Larmer

SUBSTITUTES: Mark Daly for Ian Larmer; John Paul Mone for Gerard McGuirk;
Phil McCaul for Stephen McGinnity

FERMANAGH
BACK ROW L TO R: Dara McGrath, Paul Brewster, Liam McBarron, Cormac McAdam, Tony Collins, Shaun Burns, Tom Brewster
FRONT ROW L TO R: Raymond Gallagher, Shane King, Tommy Callaghan, Paddy McGuinness, Raymond Johnson, Seán Quinn, Kieran Gallagher, Michael Lilly

MONAGHAN
BACK ROW L TO R: Joe Coyle, Frank McEneaney, Gerard McGuirk, Glen Murphy, Noel Marron, Peter Duffy, Declan Smyth, Dermot McDermott
FRONT ROW L TO R: Darren Swift, Stephen McGinnity, John Conlon, Damian Freeman, Edwin Murphy, Padraic McKenna, Ian Larmer

"Differences between a club final and a board meeting?

Well for a start they don't let you

wear a helmet into board meetings."

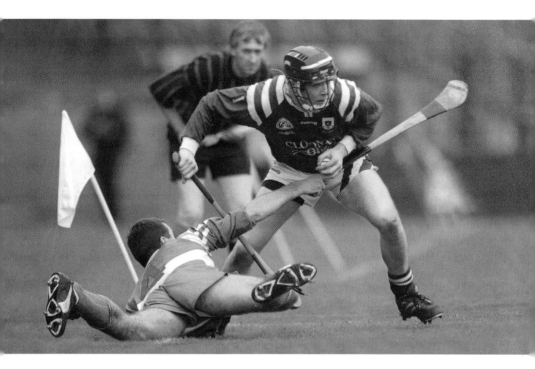

If you've got a proposal to put to your colleagues,
we're here to help you close up any chinks in your armour.

IF YOU'RE IN BUSINESS, WE'RE IN BUSINESS

SUNDAY, JUNE 6, 1999

ULSTER SENIOR FOOTBALL CHAMPIONSHIP QUARTER-FINAL

ARMAGH versus DONEGAL

MAC CUMHAILL PARK (BALLYBOFEY)

REFEREE: MICHAEL CURLEY (GALWAY)

RESULT: ARMAGH 1-12 DONEGAL 2-9 (A DRAW)

IT WAS A GAME THAT HAD AS MANY twists and turns as an old bog road! Donegal scored two goals in the opening six minutes; lost their way for the remainder of the half, scoring just two points from frees; then trailed by a point in injury time before Michael Hegarty sent over the equalising score.

Armagh goalkeeper Benny Tierney told me later that he asked a Donegal player where he might get a taxi to bring him out of Clones after the two early goals, which would surely have finished off most teams. But this Armagh side has character in abundance and their new found spirit and confidence was very much in evidence for the remainder of the game, particularly when a rejuvenated Donegal moved four points clear with nine minutes remaining. Oisín McConville converted a free for his seventh point before Paddy McKeever crashed the ball to the net to level the game for the first time in the 63rd minute. Armagh had the look of winners when Diarmuid Marsden fired them in front for the first time with a point from play but the impressive Brian Roper levelled the game. Roper is a great hearted player who never gives less than total commitment, and his enormous work-rate was instrumental in keeping Donegal's Championship hopes alive. With time almost up, Paddy McKeever latched on to a pass from McConville before scoring what appeared to be the winning point. It was not to be! Instead, Donegal substitute Michael Hegarty brought the game to a replay with the equalising point deep into injury time.

Donegal began in whirlwind style as Tony Boyle gathered a long free from Noel Hegarty before kicking the ball to the Armagh net after just three minutes play. The Armagh defence was caught out again four minutes later when John Duffy scored a fine goal following a superb pass from Adrian Sweeney. Tony Boyle added a pointed free as Donegal powered 2-1 to 0-0 ahead by the 10th minute. Incredibly, Donegal scores dried up at an alarming rate and Declan Bonner's team could only manage to score three points – all from frees – for the next forty minutes during which Armagh knocked over eight points.

Sensing an early Championship exit, Armagh introduced substitute Diarmuid Marsden in the 12th minute and the brilliant Clan Na Gael man made an immediate impact. Marsden, who failed to start the game because of injury, was involved in many of the moves, which yielded vital scores, as Armagh edged their way back, helped enormously by tremendous displays from Jarlath Burns, Kieran McGeeney, Oisín McConville and Justin McNulty. Armagh outscored Donegal by 0-5 to 0-1 for the remaining twenty-five minutes of the opening half to close the gap to just three points at the interval. McConville scored four points, three of which came from play, while Cathal O'Rourke landed Armagh's opening point after twelve minutes. Donegal led by 2-2 to 0-5 at half-time but their lead was narrowed still further shortly after the break when Paul McGrane and Diarmuid Marsden scored a point each. Armagh somehow lost their momentum as Donegal fought back and had stretched their lead to four points by the 60th minute, through points from John Duffy, Jim McGuinness, Brian Roper, Noel Hegarty and Brendan Devenney, whose score came seconds after a brilliant save by Donegal goalkeeper Tony Blake.

But Armagh's three M's, Marsden, McConville and McKeever retrieved the situation with some excellent scores that pushed them one point ahead with the game in injury time. To their credit, Donegal refused to give up and their persistence was rewarded when substitute Michael Hegarty superbly kicked over the levelling point to bring to an end a quite remarkable game. The quality of football was never of the highest quality but the closeness of the exchanges kept the pot boiling right to the very end.

SCORERS – ARMAGH: Oisín McConville 0-7; Paddy McKeever 1-1; Diarmuid Marsden 0-2; Cathal O'Rourke 0-1; Paul McGrane 0-1
DONEGAL: Tony Boyle 1-1; John Duffy 1-1; Brendan Devenney 0-2; Brian Roper 0-2; Jim McGuinness 0-1; Noel Hegarty 0-1; Michael Hegarty 0-1

ARMAGH

Benny Tierney

| Enda McNulty | Gerard Reid | Mark McNeill |
| Kieran Hughes | Kieran McGeeney | Andrew McCann |

Jarlath Burns (Captain)   Justin McNulty

| Paddy McKeever | Paul McGrane | John Rafferty |
| Peter Loughran | Cathal O'Rourke | Oisín McConville |

SUBSTITUTES: Diarmuid Marsden for Mark McNeill; John McEntee for Peter Loughran; David Wilson for Cathal O'Rourke

---

DONEGAL

Tony Blake

| Damien Diver | Mark Crossan | Eamonn Reddin |
| Noel Hegarty | Martin Coll | Niall McCready |

James Ruane   Jim McGuinness

| John Duffy | Adrian Sweeney | John Gildea |
| Brian Roper | Tony Boyle | Brendan Devenney |

SUBSTITUTES: Noel McGinley for Eamonn Reddin; Barry Ward for John Duffy; Michael Hegarty for Adrian Sweeney

ARMAGH

BACK ROW L TO R: Kieran Hughes, Andrew McCann, Paul McGrane, Justin McNulty, Benny Tierney, Cathal O'Rourke, Mark McNeill
FRONT ROW L TO R: Enda McNulty, Peter Loughran, Paddy McKeever, Kieran McGeeney, Jarlath Burns, Oisin McConville, Gerard Reid, John Rafferty

DONEGAL

BACK ROW L TO R: John Duffy, John Gildea, Brendan Devenney, James Ruane, Tony Blake, Jim McGuinness, Eamonn Reddin
FRONT ROW L TO R: Mark Crossan, Martin Coll, Niall McCready, Brian Roper, Noel Hegarty, Damien Diver, Tony Boyle, Adrian Sweeney

SUNDAY, JUNE 13, 1999

ULSTER SENIOR FOOTBALL CHAMPIONSHIP FIRST ROUND

DERRY versus CAVAN

CASEMENT PARK (BELFAST)

REFEREE: MICHAEL MC GRATH (DONEGAL)

RESULT: DERRY 2-15 CAVAN 2-15 (A DRAW)

THIS WAS A QUITE EXTRAORDINARY Ulster Championship game! Derry held a five-point advantage with less than three minutes remaining but Cavan hit back with two rapid-fire goals to edge one point clear at the end of normal time. Events on the field almost defied belief! The Derry management sent on Niall McCusker, Seamus Downey and Joe Brolly in a last-ditch attempt to retrieve the situation. And not for the first time, Brolly, who was unable to play from the start following scarlet fever, answered Derry's call with the equalising point some five minutes into injury-time. It was nothing short of a wonder score by the Dungiven man.

Cavan were handed a lifeline when the referee awarded a penalty in the 68th minute after he adjudged that Larry Reilly had been fouled. Derry argued that Reilly took a dive but their protests were all in vain and Ronan Carolan despatched the ball past Shane O'Kane. Less than two minutes later Dermot McCabe fisted a Raymond Cunningham centre into the net to put Cavan ahead and completely stun the hitherto composed Derry men. To compound Derry's misfortune, their midfielder Ronan Rocks was dismissed following an off the ball incident. Luckily for Derry, the referee allowed over five minutes injury time and ice-cool Brolly kicked the levelling point to force a replay .

Cavan played some of their best football in the opening quarter, but once Joe Cassidy scored Derry's first goal the floodgates opened. Derry took complete control and scored 1-6 in a nine-minute spell up to the 32nd minute to surge 1-8 to 0-4 ahead. It could have been considerably worse for Cavan but for the fact that Cassidy's goal bound shot hit the post in the 18th minute. Apart from Cassidy, others to score during that period of Derry dominance were Anthony Tohill, Johnny McBride, Enda Muldoon and Ronan Rocks. Cavan battled back in the closing stages of the first half with a point each from Anthony Forde and Larry Reilly to close the gap to a more manageable five points at the interval.

Just as Derry enjoyed a profitable scoring return in the second quarter, Cavan turned on the style after the break and had drawn level by the 49th minute outscoring Derry 0-6 to 0-1, with three points from Ronan Carolan and one each from Jamie Coffey, Bernard Morris and Larry Reilly.

Derry rallied with a superb pointed free from Enda Muldoon; Geoffrey McGonigle also converted a free and Henry Downey crashed the ball to the net. Carolan replied with three pointed frees to bring his tally to 0-8 but again Derry regained the initiative with two points from Tohill – both from frees – and a point from Dermot Dougan, who caused endless grief for the Cavan defence throughout the game.

Derry now had a five points cushion and the players could be forgiven for thinking their day's work was done. Not so! Cavan snatched the lead in dramatic circumstances with a goal each from Carolan and McCabe to turn the game on its head, until Brolly came to the rescue with that match-saving point!.

SCORERS – DERRY: Anthony Tohill 0-6; Joe Cassidy 1-1; Enda Muldoon 0-3; Henry Downey 1-0; Dermot Dougan 0-1; Ronan Rocks 0-1; Geoffrey McGonigle 0-1; Johnny McBride 0-1; Joe Brolly 0-1
CAVAN: Ronan Carolan 1-8; Dermot McCabe 1-1; Larry Reilly 0-2; Anthony Forde 0-1; Mickey Graham 0-1; Jamie Coffey 0-1; Bernard Morris 0-1

DERRY

Shane O'Kane

Kieran McKeever   Seán Marty Lockhart   David O'Neill

Fergal Crossan   Henry Downey   Gary Coleman

Anthony Tohill (Captain)   Ronan Rocks

Enda Muldoon   Dermot Dougan   Johnny McBride

Geoffrey McGonigle   Dermot Heaney   Joe Cassidy

SUBSITUTES: Joe Brolly for Geoffrey McGonigle; Niall McCusker for Joe Cassidy;
Seamus Downey for Johnny McBride

CAVAN

Darragh McCarthy

Ciaran Brady   Patrick Sheils   Gavin Hartin

Anthony Forde   Bernard Morris   Peter Reilly

Philip Smith   Jamie Coffey

Larry Reilly   Joe Crowe   Ronan Carolan

Jason Reilly   Dermot McCabe   Mickey Graham

SUBSTITUTES: Paul Murphy for Joe Crowe; Terry Farrelly for Patrick Sheils;
Raymond Cunningham for Jason Reilly

DERRY
BACK ROW L TO R: Geoffrey McGonigle, Dermot Heaney, Ronan Rocks, Shane O'Kane, Enda Muldoon,
Dermot Dougan, David O'Neill
FRONT ROW L TO R: Henry Downey, Anthony Tohill, Gary Coleman, Kieran McKeever, Fergal Crossan, Johnny McBride,
Seán Marty Lockhart, Joe Cassidy

CAVAN
BACK ROW L TO R: Anthony Forde, Bernard Morris, Patrick Sheils, Jamie Coffey, Ronan Carolan, Darragh McCarthy,
Joseph Crowe, Ciaran Brady
FRONT ROW L TO R: Peter Reilly, Jason Reilly, Larry Reilly, Dermot McCabe, Mickey Graham, Philip Smith, Gavin Harton

SUNDAY, JUNE 13, 1999

ULSTER SENIOR FOOTBALL CHAMPIONSHIP FIRST ROUND (REPLAY)

ARMAGH versus DONEGAL

ST. TIGHEARNACH'S PARK (CLONES)

REFEREE: MICHAEL CURLEY (GALWAY)

RESULT: ARMAGH 2-11 DONEGAL 0-12

THE STRENGTH OF ANY TEAM is in the quality of its substitutes and that was clearly evident in this rugged, physical and tension-filled Ulster Championship first round replay in Clones. Diarmuid Marsden, unable to start because of injury, and Cathal O'Rourke, who both came on as substitutes early in the second half, scored a goal each to turn the game decisively in Armagh's favour.

It was a strange game in many ways with some bizarre incidents, not least the one surrounding the dismissal of Oisín McConville late in the first half. Referee Michael Curley, following consultation with his umpire, sent McConville to the line even though it later transpired that the Crossmaglen player was not guilty of any wrongdoing when Niall McCready clashed into him. There was another peculiar development just before the start of the second half when the referee booked Donegal defender Martin Coll for a challenge on Paddy McKeever, which occurred at the end of the first half. (The Games Administration Committee later exonerated both McConville and Coll. Croke Park issued a statement: "Oisín McConville personally attended the meeting and was accompanied by County Officials. Based on evidence, including video evidence, the G.A.C. concluded that his action did not warrant a sending off. It was noted that the referee did not see the incident, which had been brought to his attention by one of his officials. Martin Coll, who received two yellow cards followed by a red card in the game, was exonerated on the basis of receiving a yellow card in error. His sending off will not be recorded against him.")

Armagh lifted their game considerably following McConville's dismissal and fine displays from Andrew McCann, Jarlath Burns, John McEntee, Gerard Reid, Paddy McKeever and Kieran McGeeney ensured Donegal were never able to widen the gap to more than four points at any stage. Such was the close nature of the exchanges that a goal for either side was likely to be crucial to the outcome and Armagh hit the net, not once, but twice to fashion a famous victory.

Armagh's sluggish start contrasted sharply with Donegal's impressive early showing, which yielded three points without reply inside eight minutes. Michael Hegarty, who scored the equalising point in the drawn game a week earlier, kicked the first point of the game in the second minute which was quickly followed by a Tony Boyle 'special' from play. Boyle increased Donegal's lead with a pointed free before Oisín McConville converted a free in the 10th minute for Armagh's opening score of the game. Jim McGuinness from a free and Michael Hegarty from play scored a point each as a dominant Donegal side deservedly surged 0-5 to 0-1 ahead after 15 minutes play. At this stage, the Armagh full back line looked anything but assured; their midfield colleagues had yet to make an impact while the forwards were coming off second best against a tigerish and well-organised Donegal defence. Donegal goalkeeper Tony Blake had to retire injured in the 13th minute and was replaced by Paul Callaghan. Oisín McConville and Tony Boyle exchanged points from frees, as the game struggled to come alive. Armagh forward John McEntee played his part in igniting the game when he scored a wonderful individual point after doggedly shaking off close-marking defenders. Armagh had a let-off soon afterwards when John Gildea got inside the defence but his fisted effort went narrowly wide. The game had now flickered to life: Boyle hit the target for his fourth point; McConville was sensationally sent-off and Paddy McKeever scored a point. But Armagh wasted good scoring chances in the closing minutes of the first-half, which enabled Donegal hold a three points advantage, 0-7 to 0-4, at the interval. Martin Coll received a yellow card before the start of the second half and was then sent off in the 44th minute for a second bookable offence. Brendan Devenney and Alan O'Neill exchanged points early in the second-half before Armagh decided it was time to introduce Diarmuid Marsden, a player of exceptional ability. Marsden's mere presence gave Armagh renewed hope!

Cathal O'Rourke, who took over the free-taking duties, and Andrew McCann scored a point each to reduce the margin to the minimum midway through the second half. Mark Crossan replied with a point for Donegal but Armagh were soon ahead for the first time when Cathal O'Rourke took a pass from Kieran Hughes and drove the ball underneath goalkeeper Paul Callaghan. John McEntee increased their lead with a point from play. Donegal reacted positively and swiftly to the setback and concerted pressure yielded three points without reply from Adrian Sweeney, Tony Boyle and John Gildea. But Armagh had no intention of capitulating and Diarmuid Marsden answered the call when he got on to the end of an excellent long ball from Cathal O'Rourke to flick the ball over the head of the advancing Paul Callaghan for the clinching goal. Armagh were now within sight of the winning post and a point each from John McEntee, Paul McGrane and Paddy McKeever saw them safely though to the next round on a 2-11 to 0-12 scoreline!

SCORERS – ARMAGH: Cathal O'Rourke 1-1; John McEntee 0-3; Diarmuid Marsden 1-0; Oisín McConville 0-2; Paddy McKeever 0-2; Paul McGrane 0-1; Alan O'Neill 0-1; Andrew McCann 0-1
DONEGAL: Tony Boyle 0-5; Michael Hegarty 0-2; Jim McGuinness 0-1; Brendan Devenney 0-1; Mark Crossan 0-1; Adrian Sweeney 0-1; John Gildea 0-1

ARMAGH

Benny Tierney

Enda McNulty   Gerard Reid   Justin McNulty

Kieran Hughes   Kieran McGeeney   Andrew McCann

Jarlath Burns (Captain)   Paul McGrane

Alan O'Neill   John McEntee   John Rafferty

David Wilson   Paddy McKeever   Oisín McConville

SUBSTITUTES: Peter Loughran for David Wilson; Diarmuid Marsden for John Rafferty; Cathal O'Rourke for Peter Loughran

DONEGAL

Tony Blake

Damien Diver   Mark Crossan   Niall McCready

Noel Hegarty   Martin Coll   Shane Carr

James Ruane   Jim McGuinness

Michael Hegarty   Adrian Sweeney   John Gildea

Brian Roper   Tony Boyle   Brendan Devenney

SUBSTITUTES: Paul Callaghan for Tony Blake; John Duffy for Michael Hegarty; Barry Ward for James Ruane

ARMAGH
BACK ROW L TO R: Paddy McKeever, Kieran Hughes, Justin McNulty, Paul McGrane, Benny Tierney, Andrew McCann, John McEntee
FRONT ROW L TO R: Enda McNulty, David Wilson, Oisín McConville, Kieran McGeeney, Jarlath Burns, Gerard Reid, Alan O'Neill, John Rafferty

DONEGAL
BACK ROW L TO R: Martin Coll, James Ruane, Tony Blake, Brendan Devenney, Jim McGuinness, John Gildea, Mark Crossan
FRONT ROW L TO R: Shane Carr, Niall McCready, Noel Hegarty, Tony Boyle, Brian Roper, Damien Diver, Michael Hegarty,
Adrian Sweeney

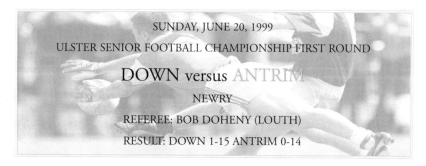

SUNDAY, JUNE 20, 1999

ULSTER SENIOR FOOTBALL CHAMPIONSHIP FIRST ROUND

DOWN versus ANTRIM

NEWRY

REFEREE: BOB DOHENY (LOUTH)

RESULT: DOWN 1-15 ANTRIM 0-14

NOT EXACTLY AN EARTH SHATTERING DISPLAY by Down but nevertheless sufficient on the day to overcome the dogged challenge of a very determined Antrim side in this
the tenth Championship meeting between the counties. Although Down controlled the
game for long periods, Antrim never gave up and battled bravely throughout in their quest
for a first Championship victory since May 1982. It is soul-destroying for Antrim footballers to lose in the first round every year and there appears to be little hope of reversing
that trend unless the current structure is altered. Like many other counties in the same
predicament, Antrim prepare assiduously for one big 'Championship' match and then it
ends, as it has done for the past seventeen years, in defeat.

As for this game, it was tough and robust, with patches of quality football played by both sides, but most especially by two Down forwards Mickey Linden and Shane Ward, who revelled in the open spaces. Linden has long been a player of genuine class and vision and he proved it once again with another excellent display. The Mayobridge man scored 1-2 as well as creating numerous scoring opportunities for his forward colleagues. Linden showed great pace in the 7th minute when he nipped inside the defence and scored what turned out to be the only goal of the game. Antrim corner-back Martin Mulholland was just about to gather the ball when Linden came in on the inside like an express train and adeptly crashed the ball to the net. That goal had the affect of settling the Down men who proceeded to dictate the pace until the half-time break. Ward scored the opening point of the game in the 1st minute and added three further points from play during the remainder of the opening half to help Down into a 1-9 to 0-6 interval lead. Ciaran McCabe was another major contributor to Down's success. The Castlewellan player was named at full forward but played for the most part as a very effective midfield link man, scoring three points in the process – two from play. Shane Mulholland was another player to impress for his all round skill and distribution.

Antrim started briskly and led by 0-2 to 0-1 after five minutes following a point from a sideline kick from Peter McCann and a close-in free from corner back Anto Finnegan. Linden's goal and impressive points from Ciaran McCabe and Shane Ward left Down 1-4 to 0-2 ahead by the 13th minute.

The game had opened up a little at this stage and Ronan Hamill and Gerard Deegan exchanged points before Kevin Madden got his name on the scoresheet with a fine point for Antrim.

Alan Molloy replaced injured Down full-back Ciaran Byrne just past the midway point of the first half and proved an able substitution for the Burren player. Although the Down defence was shaky at times, the Antrim forwards were unable to capitalise and could only muster two points in the second quarter – both from frees from Kevin Madden and Anto Finnegan. Down scored four points in that period with midfielder Brian Burns, McCabe and Ward all finding the range.

Down led at half-time by double scores, 1-9 to 0-6, but Antrim fought back gallantly in a mediocre second half and never allowed the Mourne men rest on their laurels. In a rare lapse, Down corner-forward Shane Ward shot wide with a goal chance on, early in the second half.

Paul Higgins scored a superb point off his left foot twelve minutes after the re-start and the smile on his face as he made his way upfield illustrated his delight at finding the target. Higgins was strong in defence throughout and appeared to thoroughly enjoy the game. Down had forwards that could get points from play whereas Antrim relied to a large extent on frees from Kevin Madden for their scores.

Both teams scored five points apiece between the 39th and 61st minutes but four of those scores for Antrim came from frees while Down scored four from play, including an excellent effort from Ward.

Antrim's cause was not helped by the withdrawal early in the second half of midfielder, Joe Quinn, who suffered an injury and had to leave the field.

Down's centre-half-back, Micheál Magill was sent off in the 64th minute for a second bookable offence – which forced Paddy Logan to retire injured- and Antrim took full advantage by staging a late rally, which yielded points from Gearóid Adams and Kevin Madden, who emerged as top scorer with seven points. Poor consolation for Madden and for Antrim after yet another early Championship exit!

SCORERS – DOWN: Shane Ward 0-5; Mickey Linden 1-2; Ciaran McCabe 0-3; Gerard Deegan 0-1; Micheál Magill 0-1; Brian Burns 0-1; Paul Higgins 0-1; Shane Mulholland 0-1
ANTRIM: Kevin Madden 0-7; Ronan Hamill 0-2; Anto Finnegan 0-2; John McManus 0-1; Peter McCann 0-1; Gearóid Adams 0-1

DOWN

Mickey McVeigh

Finbar Caulfield   Ciaran Byrne   Paudie Matthews

Paul Higgins   Micheál Magill   Simon Poland

Brian Burns   Seán Ward

Gerard Deegan   Shane Mulholland   James McCartan (Captain)

Mickey Linden   Ciaran McCabe   Shane Ward

SUBSTITUTES: Alan Molloy for Ciaran Byrne; Aidan Farrell for Gerard Deegan

---

ANTRIM

Donard Shannon

Martin Mulholland (Captain) Conor McKearney   Anto Finnegan

Gearóid Adams   Ciaran O'Neill   Peter McCann

Joe Quinn   Paul McErlean

Kevin Brady   Paddy Logan   Aidan Donnelly

Declan Gallagher   Ronan Hamill   Kevin Madden

SUBSTITUTES: John McManus for Aidan Donnelly; James Murphy for Joe Quinn;
Tony Convery for Paddy Logan

DOWN
BACK ROW L TO R: Micheál Magill, Brian Burns, Seán Ward, Ciaran Byrne, Mickey McVeigh, Paul Higgins, Mickey Linden, Ciaran McCabe
FRONT ROW L TO R: Paudie Mathews, James McCartan, Shane Mulholland, Shane Ward, Gerard Deegan, Finbar Caulfield, Simon Poland

SUNDAY, JUNE 20, 1999

ULSTER SENIOR FOOTBALL CHAMPIONSHIP FIRST ROUND (REPLAY)

DERRY versus CAVAN

BREFFNI PARK

REFEREE: PADDY RUSSELL (TIPPERARY)

RESULT: DERRY 2-14 CAVAN 0-5

DERRY POWERED THEIR WAY TO a fifteen points victory in this totally lop-sided replay against a Cavan team that failed dismally to reproduce the encouraging form of the controversial drawn encounter a week earlier. A thumbnail sketch of the game reveals that Cavan only scored two points from play, both in the first half while their paltry second half total amounted to just a single pointed free from Ronan Carolan. It was quite simply an awful display by Cavan and clearly the players will want to put the nightmare experience behind them as quickly as possible!

Cavan's total of five points represented the second lowest score of the entire Championship, one point more than Waterford footballers could manage against Cork in the Munster Championship game in Dungarvan on May 23.

Apart from Carolan, who accounted for four points, the only other Cavan player to score was midfielder Jamie Coffey from the Killygarry club. Coffey's point from play in the 11th minute came in response to the opening two points of the game from placed kicks by Derry midfielder Anthony Tohill. Cavan's misery started at midfield where the brilliant Tohill and Niall McCusker ruled the roost; the Derry backline was rarely troubled while the forwards picked off some excellent scores. It is very difficult to assess Derry's true worth, as a below-par Cavan team provided no more than token opposition. It was clear early on that Derry were the sharper team. Tohill landed his third free by the 13th minute while good points from play by Joe Brolly and Johnny McBride had Derry 0-5 to 0-1 ahead before the midway stage of the first half. Carolan replied with a point for Cavan before Derry struck a decisive blow! Wing-forward Enda Muldoon raced through the Cavan defence and drove the ball to the net to give Derry a commanding 1-5 to 0-2 advantage.

During the remainder of the first half, Seamus Downey and Paul McFlynn scored a point each from play for the visitors while Carolan converted two frees for a Cavan side that struggled in far too many areas of the field. Dermot McCabe had a glorious opportunity to score a goal in the 33rd minute but he blazed his shot wide. His forward colleague Mickey Graham also missed a good chance of a goal in the second half as Cavan battled to get back into the game.

Impressive Derry half backs, Henry Downey, Gary Coleman and Paul McFlynn continued to surge forward after the break; mighty Tohill remained dominant at midfield and Enda Muldoon, benefiting from good outfield play, scored three points from play to add to his first half goal.

Carolan's pointed free – Cavan's solitary score in the second half - came in the 42nd minute in reply to a point from Joe Brolly, one of seven Derry players to score.

Derry outscored a demoralised Cavan team by 1-7 to 0-1 in the second half with Dermot Dougan scoring the goal six minutes from the finish. Cavan's misery was complete when goalkeeper Damien McCusker saved Ronan Carolan's penalty kick in the 68th minute, at the expense of a '45. Derry's star forward Enda Muldoon hit the post in injury time, which was about the only slice of luck Cavan enjoyed all day long. It was Derry's best performance for some time; surely it must rate as one of Cavan's worst!

SCORERS – DERRY: Enda Muldoon 1-3; Anthony Tohill 0-4; Dermot Dougan 1-0; Paul McFlynn 0-2; Johnny McBride 0-2; Joe Brolly 0-2; Seamus Downey 0-1
CAVAN: Ronan Carolan 0-4; Jamie Coffey 0-1

DERRY

Damien McCusker

Kieran McKeever   Seán Marty Lockhart   David O'Neill

Paul McFlynn   Henry Downey   Gary Coleman

Anthony Tohill (Captain)   Niall McCusker

Dermot Heaney   Dermot Dougan   Johnny McBride

Joe Brolly   Enda Muldoon   Seamus Downey

SUBSTITUTES: Joe Cassidy for Joe Brolly; Eamonn Burns for Dermot Heaney; Fergal Crossan for Henry Downey

CAVAN

Darragh McCarthy

Anthony Forde   Patrick Sheils   Gerry Sheridan

Ciaran Brady   Peter Reilly   Bernard Morris

Jamie Coffey   Phil Smith

Raphael Rogers   Larry Reilly   Ronan Carolan

Jason Reilly   Dermot McCabe   Mickey Graham

SUBSTITUTES: Paul Murphy for Phil Smith; Raymond Cunningham for Raphael Rogers; Terry Farrelly for Jamie Coffey

DERRY
BACK ROW L TO R: David O'Neill, Dermot Heaney, Seamus Downey, Damien McCusker, Enda Muldoon, Paul McFlynn, Joe Brolly
FRONT ROW L TO R: Henry Downey, Johnny McBride, Anthony Tohill, Kieran McKeever, Gary Coleman, Niall McCusker, Dermot Dougan, Seán Marty Lockhart

CAVAN
BACK ROW L TO R: Anthony Forde, Peter Reilly, Jamie Coffey, Ronan Carolan, Patrick Sheils, Darragh McCarthy, Bernard Morris, Ciaran Brady
FRONT ROW L TO R: Larry Reilly, Gerry Sheridan, Mickey Graham, Dermot McCabe, Jason Reilly, Raphael Rogers, Philip Smith

SUNDAY, JUNE 27, 1999

ULSTER SENIOR FOOTBALL CHAMPIONSHIP QUARTER-FINAL

TYRONE versus FERMANAGH

ST. TIGHEARNACH'S PARK (CLONES)

REFEREE: BRENDAN GORMAN (ARMAGH)

RESULT: TYRONE 0-18 FERMANAGH 0-8

AFTER THEIR ENCOURAGING DISPLAY against Monaghan in the previous round, Fermanagh footballers found Tyrone in uncompromising mood in this the fifteenth Championship meeting between the counties.

Any hopes Fermanagh had of winning this game had well and truly disappeared by half-time at which stage Tyrone, with the highly impressive Adrian Cush, Peter Canavan, Eoin Gormley and Cormac McAnallen in fine form, had surged seven points ahead on a 0-9 to 0-2 scoreline.

Fermanagh settled quickly enough and dominated the game during the opening ten minutes until Cush, Canavan and company began to exert their influence. Tom Brewster converted a free in the 3rd minute, following a foul on full-forward Stephen Maguire, whose direct play and strength on the ball caused many anxious moments in the Tyrone back line. Maguire was the one player that appeared capable of breaching a tight Tyrone defence, but the Belcoo clubman was mostly fighting a lone battle up front as many of his forward colleagues were off form on the day. But the source of Fermanagh's problems was at midfield where Paul Brewster and Liam McBarron, despite a lot of strong running by both men, could never fully get to grips with Cormac McAnallen and Gerard Cavlan, who both played a key role in Tyrone's victory. Fermanagh's cause was not helped by the fact that Shane King had an uncomfortable afternoon with his free kicks and that seemed to affect his overall play. Tom Brewster was not at all as effective as he was against Monaghan and all of those factors only added to Fermanagh's woes.

After soaking up a lot of Fermanagh pressure, Adrian Cush and Mattie McGleenan scored a point each from play to give Tyrone a 0-2 to 0-1 lead by the 10th minute. Soon, it became abundantly clear that Tyrone had players that could kick scores from play, which ultimately proved the difference between the teams in the long run. Shane King pointed a free in the 12th minute but it was to be Fermanagh's last score of the first half as Tyrone took a firm hold of the game. Fermanagh, who failed to score from play in the opening half, should have been closer at the break but for some wasted opportunities from open play and frees. Cush scored his fourth point in the 27th minute and a point each from Peter Canavan, his second of the match, Eoin Gormley and McAnallen, left a much better balanced Tyrone side seven points in front at the interval. Fay Devlin, Paul McGurk, Ciaran Gourley and Colin Holmes were rock solid in defence and set up many Tyrone attacks.

McAnallen was on the mark within eleven seconds of the re-start with a superb point from play to increase Tyrone's lead, but to their credit Fermanagh refused to throw in the towel and Shane King scored their first point from play in the 38th minute. Over the next twenty minutes, Fermanagh matched Tyrone on the scoreboard, with points from Stephen Maguire, Tom Brewster, Raymond Johnson and Raymond Gallagher. Tyrone's four points in that period came from Adrian Cush, Ciaran Loughran, Peter Canavan and Gerard Cavlan, which ensured Fermanagh were kept at arms -length. Both Loughran and Brian Dooher also hit the Fermanagh posts with good efforts in the third quarter. Tyrone finished with a flurry of points and could even afford the luxury of missing a penalty in injury-time when Cavlan's shot hit the post.

SCORERS – TYRONE: Adrian Cush 0-7; Peter Canavan 0-4; Gerard Cavlan 0-2; Eoin Gormley 0-1; Cormac McAnallen 0-1; Mattie McGleenan 0-1; Ciaran Loughran 0-1; Stephen O'Neill 0-1
FERMANAGH: Shane King 0-2; Raymond Gallagher 0-2; Tom Brewster 0-2; Stephen Maguire 0-1; Raymond Johnson 0-1

TYRONE

Finbar McConnell

Fay Devlin   Chris Lawn (Captain)   Paul McGuirk

Pascal Canavan   Colin Holmes   Ciaran Gourley

Cormac McAnallen   Gerard Cavlan

Adrian Cush   Eoin Gormley   Brian Dooher

Ciaran Loughran   Mattie McGleenan   Peter Canavan

SUBSTITUTES: Stephen O'Neill for Brian Dooher; Kevin Hughes for Mattie McGleenan

FERMANAGH

Cormac McAdam

Paddy McGuinness (Captain)   Tommy Callaghan   Paul Courtney

Shaun Burns   Tony Collins   Kieran Gallagher

Paul Brewster   Liam McBarron

Raymond Johnson   Tom Brewster   Dara McGrath

Raymond Gallagher   Stephen Maguire   Shane King

SUBSTITUTES: Neil Cox for Tony Collins; Colm Courtney for Dara McGrath; Colm Bradley for Shane King

TYRONE
BACK ROW L TO R: Paul Devlin, Seamus McCallen, Adrian Cush, Gerard Cavlan, Eoin Gormley, Cormac McAnallen, Mattie McGleenan, Finbar McConnell, Stephen O'Neill, Kevin Hughes, Brian Dooher, Pascal McConnell, Ciaran McBride
FRONT ROW L TO R: Ronan Mc Garrity, Ciaran Loughran, Peter Canavan, Chris Lawn, Colin Holmes, Paul McGurk, Ciaran Gourley, Fay Devlin, Pascal Canavan; SITTING IN FRONT: Michael McGee

FERMANAGH
BACK ROW L TO R: Dara McGrath, Paul Brewster, Liam McBarron, Cormac McAdam, Stephen Maguire, Tony Collins, Tom Brewster, Paul Courtney
FRONT ROW L TO R: Raymond Gallagher, Tommy Callaghan, Shane King, Paddy McGuiness, Raymond Johnson, Kieran Gallagher, Shaun Burns

SUNDAY, JULY 4, 1999

ULSTER SENIOR FOOTBALL CHAMPIONSHIP SEMI-FINAL

ARMAGH versus DERRY

ST. TIGHEARNACH'S PARK (CLONES)

REFEREE: JOHN BANNON (LONGFORD)

RESULT: ARMAGH 1-10 DERRY 0-12

THE EXPRESSION OF JOY ON THE FACE of Armagh forward Diarmuid Marsden after he kicked over the lead point in injury time contrasted sharply with the look of sheer despair on the face of Derry wing-back Paul McFlynn after his effort for the equalising point sailed narrowly wide. It looked like it was going to be just another in the litany of hard luck stories for Armagh when Derry hit over four unanswered points to move one point ahead, as the game entered the final few minutes. But things have changed in the Orchard County! There is now a great self-belief among the players who wear the Armagh jersey and this was best epitomised by the manner in which the defence soaked up the Derry pressure in the final quarter and then struck back defiantly for match-winning scores.

Flynn's wide summed up Derry's day! Too many of their players wasted good scoring opportunities, which proved extremely costly for the defending champions.

The game was underway barely twenty seconds when Paul McGrane grounded Derry captain Anthony Tohill and referee John Bannon immediately awarded a penalty. Derry defender Gary Coleman took the kick, which was tipped over the crossbar by Armagh goalkeeper Benny Tierney. Paddy McKeever sent over the equalising point from a free before Joe Brolly edged Derry ahead again with a fine point from play. As it transpired, it was to be Brolly's only score of the game. The star Dungiven player, who untypically missed some frees and also hit the post in the course of the game, was never allowed any space to showcase his silken skills and Joe Cassidy eventually replaced him. Paul McGrane made amends for conceding the early penalty by scoring two points from play to edge Armagh ahead for the first time in the 8th minute. Armagh forward Alan O'Neill had to retire injured and Cathal O'Rourke took his place after a lengthy stoppage in play. O'Rourke, who was unlucky to see his shot come off the post immediately after his introduction, went on to score two points and made a valuable contribution in general play. Seamus Downey levelled the game for the third time with a point from play in the 15th minute and Tohill then pointed two frees for the Derry men.

Armagh hit back quickly when the speedy Oisín McConville took a pass from John Rafferty before racing through and despatching the ball to the Derry net past goalkeeper Damien McCusker.

O'Rourke and Seamus Downey swapped points before the break to leave Armagh ahead at half-time by a single point on a 1-4 to 0-6 scoreline. O'Rourke was deprived of a goal by a superb save from Derry goalkeeper Damien McCusker near the end of the opening half. There was little free flowing football in that first half and both sides conceded numerous frees. Much of Derry's positive out-field work came to nought, as the forwards squandered far too many scoring chances.

Athough Oisín McConville stretched Armagh's lead within a minute of the re-start, it was Derry who created the most chances, but with limited reward. The Armagh defence, backboned by Kieran McGeeney, tackled with ferocity and Derry had to try their luck from a distance. Joe Brolly from a free, Seamus Downey and Paul McFlynn all shot wide in quick succession. McFlynn scored Derry's first point of the second half in the 43rd minute but Oisín McConville replied with a point for a fired-up Armagh side. Tony McEntee replaced John Rafferty on the Armagh team; Brolly hit the post from a free and Gary Coleman was off target from play as Derry wasted good chances. Armagh had better luck in front of the posts and Paddy McKeever's fisted point put the Orchard County men 1-7 to 0-7 ahead by the 49th minute.

Derry stormed back into the game and outscored Armagh by 0-4 to 0-1 over the next 15 minutes to level the game for the fourth time. Tohill, who produced another dominant display to give his side a distinct advantage at midfield, was to the fore in Derry's comeback, scoring two points from frees, while Johnny McBride and Dermot Dougan also hit over points. Diarmuid Marsden scored a point from play for Armagh during that spell of

Derry pressure.

Derry voices rang out around Clones when Joe Cassidy, who had earlier replaced Brolly, kicked over the lead point in the 65th minute. Perhaps, on other days, Derry would have consolidated their position but instead a spirited Armagh side dug deep and O'Rourke shot over the equalising point from a free. There was still more drama to unfold: Marsden edged Armagh in front; McFlynn, one of Derry's star players on the day, let fly but his effort sailed agonisingly wide and all of Armagh celebrated a famous victory.

SCORERS – ARMAGH: Oisín McConville 1-2; Diarmuid Marsden 0-2; Paul McGrane 0-2; Paddy McKeever 0-2; Cathal O'Rourke 0-2
DERRY: Anthony Tohill 0-4; Seamus Downey 0-2; Joe Brolly 0-1; Gary Coleman 0-1; Paul McFlynn 0-1; Dermot Dougan 0-1; Johnny McBride 0-1; Joe Cassidy 0-1

ARMAGH

Benny Tierney

| Enda McNulty | Gerard Reid | Justin McNulty |
| Kieran Hughes | Kieran McGeeney | Andrew McCann |

Jarlath Burns (Captain)   Paul McGrane

| Paddy McKeever | John McEntee | John Rafferty |
| Alan O'Neill | Diarmuid Marsden | Oisín McConville |

SUBSTITUTES: Cathal O'Rourke for Alan O'Neill; Tony McEntee for John Rafferty

---

DERRY

Damien McCusker

| Fergal Crossan | Seán Marty Lockhart | Kieran McKeever |
| Paul McFlynn | Henry Downey | Gary Coleman |

Anthony Tohill (Captain)   Niall McCusker

| Dermot Heaney | Dermot Dougan | Johnny McBride |
| Joe Brolly | Enda Muldoon | Seamus Downey |

SUBSTITUTES: Declan Bateson for Seamus Downey; Joe Cassidy for Joe Brolly

ARMAGH
BACK ROW L TO R: Andrew McCann, Justin McNulty, Kieran Hughes, Paul McGrane, Benny Tierney, John McEntee
FRONT ROW L TO R: Enda McNulty, Alan O'Neill, Paddy McKeever, Oisín McConville, Kieran McGeeney, Jarlath Burns, Diarmuid Marsden, Gerard Reid, John Rafferty

DERRY
BACK ROW L TO R: Seamus Downey, Dermot Dougan, Dermot Heaney, Damien McCusker, Enda Muldoon, Paul McFlynn, Joe Brolly
FRONT ROW L TO R: Johnny McBride, Seán Marty Lockhart, Henry Downey, Gary Coleman, Anthony Tohill, Kieran McKeever, Niall McCusker, Fergal Crossan

SUNDAY, JULY 11, 1999

ULSTER SENIOR FOOTBALL CHAMPIONSHIP SEMI-FINAL

DOWN versus TYRONE

CASEMENT PARK (BELFAST)

REFEREE: PAT MC ENEANEY (MONAGHAN)

RESULT: DOWN 2-14 TYRONE 0-15

NOT EVEN DOWN'S MOST ARDENT SUPPORTER would have envisaged this result nine minutes before half-time when Tyrone were in full flow and held the upperhand completely. Conversely, Down were finding it very difficult to cope with the sheer pace of the Tyrone forwards who picked off some excellent scores. Indeed Tyrone could have been further ahead but for some wasted chances which, if converted, could have knocked Down's comeback on the head.

It was looking bleak for Down when they trailed by six points after twenty-six minutes, but the trend of the game changed dramatically soon afterwards. Firstly, twice All-Ireland winning medalist, Ross Carr, took over the free taking duties from Shane Mulholland, who was having no luck with placed kicks, and Down prospered before the break. Missed frees apart, Mulholland had an excellent game at centre-half-forward. The impressive Shane Ward sent over a point to settle the Mournemen, who had earlier missed a number of good scoring opportunities. Then Carr, who had opted to come out of retirement a few weeks before the game, converted two frees before Paul Higgins kicked the ball over the bar to close within two points of Tyrone by the half-time break. Paudie Matthews played superbly when introduced in place of Ciaran Byrne in the Down defence near the end of the first half. Down weathered the storm and then went on to outscore Tyrone by 2-7 to 0-6 in a second half display that represented Down football at its best. It was a superb showing by Down and great credit is due to long-serving manager Peter McGrath for masterminding the victory.

Micheál Magill, who took over the captaincy from the injured James McCartan, along with Finbar Caulfield, who curbed the threat of Peter Canavan, were both outstanding in a much-improved Down defence in the second half. Brian Burns and Alan Molloy produced dominant displays at midfield while Mickey Linden and Ciaran McCabe led a less than assured Tyrone defence, minus injured captain, Chris Lawn, a merry dance. And yet it had all begun so positively for the Tyrone team!

Brian Dooher and Adrian Cush scored two early points as Tyrone settled to their task with a vigour that suggested a team determined to wipe out the opposition. Peter Canavan then added two further points for Tyrone before Shane Ward opened the scoring for Down with a point from play in the 9th minute.

Six Tyrone players, including defender Ronan McGarrity and midfielder Gerard Cavlan, had found the target by the 26th minute, as Down struggled to keep in touch. But a flurry of points left Down in a more favourable position at the half-time break, although facing the breeze in the second half.

Brian Dooher scored the first point of the second half to increase Tyrone's lead but not long afterwards the game took a dramatic turn. Finbar McConnell brought off a superb save only for Ciaran McCabe to gather the ball and score an excellent goal to level the match for the first time. Although Mickey Linden and Dooher swapped points, the game had now swung decisively in Down's favour. The Tyrone forwards were unable to make any headway against a dominant Down defence and the writing was on the wall when McCabe sent over the lead point in the 45th minute. Down had stretched their lead to three points when McCabe scored his second goal to effectively end the game as a contest.

Ciaran McCabe brought his tally to 2-3 with a pointed free before the finish to complete an outstanding individual display on a day when Down had many heroes at Casement Park.

SCORERS – DOWN: Ciaran McCabe 2-3; Mickey Linden 0-3; Ross Carr 0-3; Shane Mulholland 0-2; Shane Ward 0-2; Paul Higgins 0-1;
TYRONE: Adrian Cush 0-4; Peter Canavan 0-3; Brian Dooher 0-3; Gerard Cavlan 0-2; Eoin Gormley 0-1; Ronan McGarrity 0-1; Ciaran Loughran 0-1

DOWN

Mickey McVeigh

Finbar Caulfield   Micheál Magill (Captain)   Ciaran Byrne

Paul Higgins   Seán Ward   Simon Poland

Brian Burns   Alan Molloy

Gerard Deegan   Shane Mulholland   Ross Carr

Mickey Linden   Ciaran McCabe   Shane Ward

SUBSTITUTES: Paudie Matthews for Ciaran Byrne

TYRONE

Finbar McConnell

Fay Devlin   Ronan McGarrity   Paul McGurk

Pascal Canavan   Colin Holmes   Ciaran Gourley

Cormac McAnallen   Gerard Cavlan

Adrian Cush   Eoin Gormley   Brian Dooher

Ciaran Loughran   Mattie McGleenan   Peter Canavan

SUBSTITUTES: Stephen Lawn for Cormac McAnallen; Paul Devlin for Paul McGurk;
Stephen O'Neill for Ciaran Loughran

DOWN
BACK ROW L TO R: Paul Higgins, Finbar Caulfield, Alan Molloy, Simon Poland, Mickey McVeigh, Ciaran Byrne, Mickey Linden, Brian Burns
FRONT ROW L TO R: Ross Carr, Shane Ward, Gerard Deegan, Micheál Magill, Shane Mulholland, Seán Ward, Ciaran McCabe

TYRONE
BACK ROW L TO R: Paul Devlin, Adrian Cush, Ronan McGarrity, Cormac McAnallen, Finbar McConnell, Colin Holmes, Gerard Cavlan, Mattie McGleenan, Pascal McConnell, Eoin Gormley, Ciaran McBride
FRONT ROW L TO R: Stephen Lawn, Ciaran Gourley, Paul McGurk, Michael McGee, Ciaran Loughran, Peter Canavan, Fay Devlin, Kevin Hughes, Pascal Canavan, Brian Dooher, Seamus McCallen
SITTING: Richard Thornton, Stephen O'Neill

SUNDAY, AUGUST 1, 1999

ULSTER SENIOR FOOTBALL CHAMPIONSHIP FINAL

ARMAGH versus DOWN

ST. TIGHEARNACH'S PARK (CLONES)

REFEREE: PADDY RUSSELL (TIPPERARY)

RESULT: ARMAGH 3-12 DOWN 0-10

INSPIRATIONAL CAPTAIN JARLATH BURNS summed up best of all what the win meant to the people of Armagh in his emotional after-match speech to thousands of jubilant supporters converged on the pitch beneath the Stand. Midfielder Burns, a player of immense stature and presence, captured the mood of a never-to-be-forgotten occasion when he said: "today Armagh footballers stood up and were counted." And that is precisely what happened! It was Armagh's first Ulster title since their three-point victory over Fermanagh in the 1982 Final and it was achieved in an authoritative and decisive manner by a talented team brimful of confidence. It was a performance of real quality by an Armagh team that possessed far too much strength, mobility and scoring prowess for a disappointing Down side that never functioned with the fluency evident against Tyrone in the semi-final.

Diarmuid Marsden and Oisín McConville, later described to me by Jarlath Burns as 'two great Irish warriors', between them dismantled a porous Down defence with incisive running and clinical finishing. It was clear Marsden had the measure of corner back, Finbar Caulfield from early on and the brilliant Clan Na Gael man set up McConville for the first goal of the game in the 12th minute. McConville's finish was exquisite as Armagh surged 1-3 to 0-2 ahead. Earlier, McConville had scored two points while Marsden also found the target with a delightful point from play. During that period, Ciaran McCabe landed two frees for the Down men and shortly after McConville's goal, both Brian Burns and Ross Carr also hit over points.

Armagh defenders closed down every space in the early stages, with just Marsden and McConville up front, a ploy that worked very effectively for the Orchard County. Down persisted with the tactic of sending the ball to Mickey Linden and even though the '1994 Footballer of the Year' won plenty of good possession, scores were hard to come by as Armagh packed their defence.

The game was still delicately poised when Marsden collected a long delivery from full-back Gerard Reid and crashed the ball to the net for a superb goal. McConville tacked on two further points to leave Armagh 2-5 to 0-4 ahead by the 26th minute. Down came back strongly in the closing stages of the half and the Armagh backs were put to the pin of their collars to withstand the constant pressure, which yielded two points from frees by

Shane Mulholland.

The expected Down revival never materialised in the second half and instead Armagh tightened their grip on the game and picked of some excellent scores from McConville, Marsden and Paul McGrane. Down substitute Gregory McCartan scored a fine point from play but Armagh effectively clinched victory when McConville converted a penalty midway through the second half after Paddy McKeever was fouled. Justin McNulty, Gerard Reid and Enda McNulty played superbly in the full back line while half backs Kieran Hughes, Kieran McGeeney, a tower of strength at centre-half-back, and Andrew McCann confidently snuffed out many a Down attack before launching one of their own. Mighty captain Jarlath Burns and Paul McGrane continually helped out in defence as well as winning vital possession at midfield. Marsden and McConville were the outstanding duo in attack, but there were solid contributions also from Paddy McKeever, John McEntee, John Rafferty and Cathal O'Rourke.

Down could only manage four points in the second half – one each from play from McCartan and Shane Ward and two frees by Mulholland – while Armagh scored 1-7 with the final two points scored by brothers John and Tony McEntee. Down's misery was complete when full-back Seán Ward was sent off late in the game for a second bookable offence. James McCartan, who was unable to line out because of injury, made an appearance late in the second half and tried very hard to lift his team, but at that stage Armagh had matters well under control. It was Armagh's first ever victory over Down in an Ulster Final on a day that will be remembered for the marvellous displays of Oisín McConville, who scored no less than 2-7, and the magnificent Diarmuid Marsden. It was wonderful to see one of the true greats of Armagh football, Ger Houlahan make a brief appearance at the end to gain just reward for wonderful service to the county in leaner days.

SCORERS – ARMAGH: Oisín McConville 2-7; Diarmuid Marsden 1-2; Paul McGrane 0-1; John McEntee 0-1; Tony McEntee 0-1
DOWN: Shane Mulholland 0-4; Ciaran McCabe 0-2; Brian Burns 0-1; Ross Carr 0-1; Gregory McCartan 0-1; Shane Ward 0-1

ARMAGH

Benny Tierney

| Enda McNulty | Gerard Reid | Justin McNulty |
| Kieran Hughes | Kieran McGeeney | Andrew McCann |

Jarlath Burns (Captain)   Paul McGrane

| Paddy McKeever | John McEntee | John Rafferty |
| Cathal O'Rourke | Diarmuid Marsden | Oisín McConville |

SUBSTITUTES: Tony McEntee for John Rafferty; Ger Houlahan for Cathal O'Rourke

DOWN

Mickey McVeigh

Finbar Caulfield   Seán Ward   Paudie Matthews

Paul Higgins   Micheál Magill (Captain)   Simon Poland

Brian Burns   Alan Molloy

Ross Carr   Shane Mulholland   Gerard Deegan

Mickey Linden   Ciaran McCabe   Shane Ward

SUBSTITUTES: Gregory McCartan for Alan Molloy; Aidan Farrell for Gerard Deegan
James McCartan for Mickey Linden

ARMAGH
BACK ROW L TO R: Ger Houlahan, David Kelly, Steven McDonnell, John Donaldson, Tony McEntee, Paul McGrane, Justin McNulty, Andrew McCann, Benny Tierney, Mark Campbell, Kieran Hughes, Diarmuid Marsden, Cathal O'Rourke, John McEntee, Mark McNeill
FRONT ROW L TO R: James Byrne, Alan O'Neill, Des Mackin, Enda McNulty, David Wilson, Aidan O'Rourke, Kieran McGeeney, Jarlath Burns, Oisín McConville, Paddy McKeever, Gerard Reid, John Rafferty, Peter Loughran

DOWN
BACK ROW L TO R: Finbar Caulfield, Paul Higgins, Brian Burns, Mickey McVeigh, Seán Ward, Mickey Linden
FRONT ROW L TO R: Ross Carr, Ciaran McCabe, Gerard Deegan, Simon Poland, Micheal Magill, Shane Ward, Alan Molloy, Shane Mulholland. MISSING FROM PHOTO: Paudie Matthews

SUNDAY, AUGUST 22, 1999

ALL-IRELAND SENIOR FOOTBALL SEMI-FINAL

CORK versus MAYO

CROKE PARK

REFEREE: JOHN BANNON (LONGFORD)

RESULT: CORK 2-12 MAYO 0-12

CORK QUALIFIED FOR THE ALL-IRELAND football final as Mayo suffered more disappointment on big match day in Croke Park. Mayo manager John Maughan had hoped his team could make up for bitter losses in '96 and '97 but again luck deserted the Connacht Champions, who must surely rate as the unlucky team of the nineties at All-Ireland level. Mayo had shown good form throughout the Connacht Championship campaign but despite a brave effort were unable to see off the challenge of a very determined and highly skilful Cork side that refused to panic following a poor start.

It had all begun so well for Mayo who raced into a 0-6 to 0-1 lead by the 18th minute through a combination of superb play and some great point scoring. But it turned Cork's way once the highly impressive Philip Clifford scored the opening goal of the game in the 26th minute. The sides were level at half-time and somehow one sensed that Mayo had let the initiative slip following their dream start that saw them surge five points clear. Cork began to control midfield and Mayo found it very difficult to win the quality possession required to keep their challenge alive. The Cork defence battened down the hatches after the early onslaught; midfield played superbly while the forwards continually troubled the beleaguered Mayo back line. Philip Clifford scored 1-4 to underline his prowess as a forward of exceptional ability while Anthony Lynch was excellent in defence.

James Horan scored the opening point while Kieran McDonald and Colm McManamon tacked on a point each before Don Davis, impressive throughout, kick-started Cork's challenge with a point from play. But there was no stopping Mayo at this juncture and further points from Horan, Maurice Sheridan and Kenneth Mortimer served to underline their dominance. The Cork defence looked disjointed as Mayo fired over the points to consolidate their dominace in attack as well as in defence. The game changed once Seán Óg Ó hAilpín and Ronan McCarthy switched positions in the Cork defence. Cork began to look more assured and Podsie O'Mahony kicked over two points and Philip Clifford scored a vital goal to level the game for the first time. All Mayo's early work had been wiped out and suddenly Cork had matters under control. Mark O'Sullivan put Cork in front for the first time in the 31st minute but Kieran McDonald levelled the match coming up to half-time.

Cork, having played against the breeze, were much happier with the half-time scoreline and their second half display bore all the hallmarks of a team full of confidence. Mayo to their credit never gave up and Horan's third point in the 50th minute pushed the Connacht Champions 1-8 to 0-10 ahead. Mayo were unlucky in that the usually very reliable Maurice Sheridan was off target from a number of frees which exacerbated their problems. Cork midfielders Nicholas Murphy and Micheál O'Sullivan were strong and forceful and Mayo introduced Pat Fallon in an attempt to limit their effectiveness. Philip Clifford was a thorn in the Mayo defence all through and his fourth point of the second-half pushed Cork 1-11 to 0-11 in front with less than seven minutes remaining. To round off a very satisfactory individual display, Clifford passed to Fionán Murray for Cork's second goal on the brink of full-time to give the Munster Champions plenty of breathing space as the game petered out. James Horan and Kieran McDonald scored three points each for Mayo in a game that Cork deserved to win after recovering from a shaky start before finally stamping their authority on proceedings. Manager Larry Tompkins has instilled great character into this Cork side as evidenced in their League title success and now this well-merited All-Ireland semi final win.

SCORERS – CORK: Philip Clifford 1-4; Fionán Murray 1-1; Podsie O'Mahony 0-3; Don Davis 0-2; Joe Kavanagh 0-1; Mark O'Sullivan 0-1
MAYO: James Horan 0-3; Kieran McDonald 0-3; Maurice Sheridan 0-3; Kenneth Mortimer 0-1; Colm McManamon 0-1; David Brady 0-1

CORK

Kevin O'Dwyer

| Ronan McCarthy | Seán Óg Ó hAilpín | Anthony Lynch |
| Ciarán O'Sullivan | Owen Sexton | Martin Cronin |

| Nicholas Murphy | | Micheál O'Sullivan |

| Micheál Cronin | Joe Kavanagh | Podsie O'Mahony |
| Philip Clifford (Captain) | Don Davis | Mark O'Sullivan |

SUBSTITUTES: Fachtna Collins for Micheál Cronin; Fionán Murray for Podsie O'Mahony; Brendan Jer O'Sullivan for Philip Clifford

---

MAYO

Peter Burke

| Aidan Higgins | Kevin Cahill | Gordon Morley |
| Fergal Costello | David Heaney | Alan Roche |

| James Nallen | | David Brady |

| Kieran McDonald | Kenneth Mortimer (Captain) | Colm McManamon |
| Maurice Sheridan | James Horan | David Nestor |

SUBSTITUTES: Pat Fallon for Gordon Morley; John Casey for Kenneth Mortimer; Liam McHale for David Nestor

CORK
BACK ROW L TO R: Mark O'Sullivan, Micheál O'Sullivan, Ronan McCarthy, Nicholas Murphy, Seán Óg Ó hAilpín, Micheál Cronin, Ciarán O'Sullivan
FRONT ROW L TO R: Joe Kavanagh, Eoin Sexton, Martin Cronin, Kevin O'Dwyer, Philip Clifford, Anthony Lynch, Podsie O'Mahony, Don Davis

MAYO
BACK ROW L TO R: Kevin Cahill, James Horan, Kieran McDonald, Maurice Sheridan, Peter Burke, David Brady, David Heaney, James Nallen
FRONT ROW L TO R: Gordon Morley, Alan Roche, Fergal Costello, Kenneth Mortimer, Aidan Higgins, Colm McManamon, David Nestor

SUNDAY, AUGUST 29, 1999

ALL-IRELAND SENIOR FOOTBALL SEMI-FINAL

MEATH versus ARMAGH

CROKE PARK

REFEREE: PADDY RUSSELL (TIPPERARY)

RESULT: MEATH 0-15 ARMAGH 2-5

MEATH AND CORK, WHO CONTESTED the first final of the decade, will now meet in the last All-Ireland Football decider of the Millenium on Sunday September 26 in Croke Park. Meath booked their place in the final with a deserved 0-15 to 2-5 victory over Armagh in what was an interesting, if not exactly awe-inspiring contest. Armagh scored just once in the second half as Meath hit over seven points in a game that saw the Ulster Champions reduced to fourteen players when full-back Gerard Reid was sent off for a second bookable offence in the 54th minute. Armagh never recovered from that setback as Meath pulled away scoring five points without reply to complete a solid, workmanlike performance.

Meath, through points from Trevor Giles, Evan Kelly and Donal Curtis, had moved 0-3 to 0-1 ahead by the 11th minute after Paddy McKeever had opened the scoring for Armagh after just three minutes play.

A brilliantly finished goal by Diarmuid Marsden in the 15th minute inspired Armagh and a second goal from wing-back, Kieran Hughes nine minutes later gave Armagh a three points advantage, 2-1 to 0-4 by the 24th minute. Meath battled back and the margin was reduced to just two points at the interval, Armagh 2-4, Meath 0-8. Among the highlights of the closing stages of the first half were two superb points from play for Armagh by Paddy McKeever. Seven Meath players scored in the first half, Trevor Giles, Evan Kelly, Donal Curtis, Enda McManus, Nigel Nestor, Graham Geraghty and Ray Magee as opposed to three for Armagh, namely Paddy McKeever, Diarmuid Marsden and Kieran Hughes. Meath suffered a severe blow past the midway point of the first half when Ollie Murphy had to be stretchered off injured.

Any chance Armagh had of winning this game disappeared between the 45th and 49th minute when they shot five wides at a stage when the team was moving well and in control. Trevor Giles scored the first point of the second half but that was cancelled out by a Paddy McKeever free in the 43rd minute. Incredibly, Armagh failed to score again as Meath took advantage of every slip up by the Ulster Champions. Those points from Giles and McKeever were the only scores of the third quarter, but once Gerard Reid received his marching orders, Meath took control with confidence. The Leinster Champions went in front for only the second time with ten minutes remaining through points from Ray Magee, Trevor Giles and the lead score from Evan Kelly. Meath are renowned for their ability to put teams away given half a chance and they showed their class in the closing stages with good points from Donal Curtis, Trevor Giles and Evan Kelly to sweep to victory on a 0-15 to 2-5 scoreline.

SCORERS – MEATH: Trevor Giles 0-5; Evan Kelly 0-3; Ray Magee 0-2; Donal Curtis 0-2; Enda McManus 0-1; Nigel Nestor 0-1; Graham Geraghty 0-1
ARMAGH: Paddy McKeever 0-4; Diarmuid Marsden 1-1; Kieran Hughes 1-0

MEATH

Cormac Sullivan

Mark O'Reilly   Darren Fay   Cormac Murphy

Hank Traynor   Enda McManus   Paddy Reynolds

Nigel Crawford   John McDermott

Evan Kelly   Trevor Giles   Nigel Nestor

Ollie Murphy   Graham Geraghty (Captain)   Donal Curtis

SUBSTITUTE: Ray Magee for Ollie Murphy

ARMAGH

Benny Tierney

Enda McNulty   Gerard Reid   Justin McNulty

Kieran Hughes   Kieran McGeeney   Andrew McCann

Jarlath Burns (Captain)   Paul McGrane

Tony McEntee   John Donaldson   Diarmuid Marsden

Paddy McKeever   John McEntee   Oisín McConville

SUBSTITUTES: Cathal O'Rourke for John McEntee; Alan O'Neill for Paul McGrane

MEATH
BACK ROW L TO R: Trevor Giles, John McDermott, Graham Geraghty, Darren Fay, Cormac Sullivan, Nigel Crawford, Hank Traynor, Nigel Nestor, Cormac Murphy
FRONT ROW L TO R: Mark O'Reilly, Donal Curtis, Evan Kelly, Paddy Reynolds, Ollie Murphy, Enda McManus

ARMAGH
BACK ROW L TO R: David Kelly, Ger Houlahan, Mark Campbell, Andrew McCann, John McEntee, John Donaldson, Paul McGrane, Benny Tierney, Justin McNulty, Kieran Hughes, Cathal O'Rourke, Peter Loughran, Aidan O'Rourke, Mark McNeill
FRONT ROW L TO R: James Byrne, Steven McDonnell, Des Mackin, Enda McNulty, Oisín McConville, Paddy McKeever, Kieran McGeeney, Jarlath Burns, Diarmuid Marsden, Gerard Reid, Tony McEntee, David Wilson, Alan O'Neill, John Rafferty

The secret of being Ireland's leading food company...

(we listen to our customers)

Glanbia is the new name for Ireland's number one food company. With an annual turnover of approximately €2·6 billion and 8,000 employees, our Group is one of the world's leading dairy companies with strong positions in selected consumer and global ingredients markets, in addition to significant interests in the meats sector.

From our operations in Ireland, UK, USA and Belgium, we serve markets across the EU, USA, Asia, Latin America and Africa.

At home in Ireland, Glanbia is best known to consumers for our range of market-leading food brands, including Avonmore, Kilmeaden, Petits Filous, Premier, Roscrea and Yoplait.

Glanbia is committed to being an internationally competitive and globally relevant food company. We will deliver value for all our stakeholders through excellence in market knowledge, innovation, uncompromising quality, operational efficiency and great customer service.

100% IRISH
Supermac's
Family Restaurants
Where you're always a winner!
Supermac's Fast Food
Tasty & Tempting
TASTY & TEMPTING
Branches Nationwide

ALL-IRELAND SENIOR HURLING CHAMPIONSHIP FINAL

CORK versus KILKENNY

CROKE PARK

REFEREE: PAT O'CONNOR (LIMERICK).

RESULT: CORK 0-13, KILKENNY 0-12

THE WEEK BEFORE THE GAME a number of former Kilkenny players voiced concern at the level of confidence amongst supporters. But, manager Brian Cody was adamant that his team did not lose the All-Ireland hurling final through 'over-confidence.' Either way, it suited Cork to perfection to be so widely regarded as underdogs. It was a day for Jimmy Barry-Murphy to celebrate the greatest of all his many achievements in sport, a day to exorcise a lot of bad memories for him and supporters.

And, on a day that Brian Corcoran climbed his Everest with such style and panache, all six Cork backs, along with goalkeeper Donal Óg Cusack, combined to produce a masterful performance. Combined with the wastage of possession, which undermined Kilkenny's challenge to a serious degree, it was what ultimately decided the destination of the Liam McCarthy Cup.

Both sides experienced difficulty in scoring through the first half, but particularly in the opening quarter. That was hardly surprising in view of the unfavourable conditions. Although playing against the wind, Cork were three points ahead by the 17th minute. Two minutes later came Kilkenny's opening score from a Henry Shefflin free, which followed nine wides. Within another four minutes the sides were level at 0-4 each.

At this stage of the game, Cork were doing unexpectedly well in the half-forward line with Timmy McCarthy very effective. Fergal McCormack's hard work was also paying dividends. More surprisingly, Kilkenny were not penetrating to the level anticipated from them in their half-forward line. Brian McEvoy won a lot of possession but missed a number of chances. Brian Corcoran was a dominant force throughout at centre half back for Cork while Seán Óg Ó hAilpín kept a close eye on DJ Carey.

The more the game progressed, the more the Cork backs grew in confidence. And, there was no appreciable improvement from the Kilkenny attack – in terms of the openings they created or the chances they finished off. Kilkenny didn't have a lot to show for their efforts. Likewise, individual Cork forwards spurned good opportunities of scores.

Kilkenny took the lead for the first time, in the 28th minute. The score came from John Power, when D.J. Carey passed to him. And, it was this score which had the favourites ahead at half-time, 0-5 to 0-4.

Their lead lasted no more than 13 seconds, before second half substitute Alan Browne pointed for Cork. Nevertheless, it was Kilkenny who dictated the trend of the game over the next fifteen minutes. Firstly, they regained the lead through a Charlie Carter point - D.J. Carey supplying the pass, and then scored another three points without reply to move into a strong position. Cork substitute Kevin Murray scored a marvellous point from an angled shot. After that, Cork came storming back, sensing victory.

The move of Timmy McCarthy to midfield proved a master-stroke by the management. Mark Landers, a fortnight earlier considered doubtful after keyhole surgery on his knee, had played himself to a standstill and Kevin Murray had come in for him at full-forward. It was a day when McCarthy finally 'delivered' on his promise as he proceeded to win vital possession.

Seanie McGrath hit over two glorious points to bring Cork level by the 62nd minute before Ben O'Connor and Joe Deane followed with two invaluable scores over the next five minutes.

It was still anybody's game, especially after Henry Shefflin narrowed the margin to a point in the 67th minute but Cork's outstanding defence held firm until the final whistle.

SCORERS: CORK – Timmy McCarthy 0-3; Joe Deane 0-3; Seanie McGrath 0-3; Mark Landers 0-1; Alan Browne 0-1; Kevin Murray 0-1; Ben O'Connor 0-1.
KILKENNY – Henry Shefflin 0-5; Andy Comerford 0-2; Charlie Carter 0-2; Brian McEvoy 0-1; John Power 0-1; Denis Byrne 0-1.

CORK

Donal Óg Cusack

Fergal Ryan   Diarmuid O'Sullivan   John Browne

Wayne Sherlock   Brian Corcoran   Seán Óg Ó hAilpín

Mark Landers (Captain)   Mickey O'Connell

Timmy McCarthy   Fergal McCormack   Neil Ronan

Seanie McGrath   Joe Deane   Ben O'Connor

SUBSTITUTES: Alan Browne for Neil Ronan; Kevin Murray for Mark Landers.

KILKENNY

James McGarry

Philip Larkin   Canice Brennan   Willie O'Connor

Michael Kavanagh   Pat O'Neill   Peter Barry

Andy Comerford   Denis Byrne (Captain)

D.J. Carey   John Power   Brian McEvoy

Ken O'Shea   Henry Shefflin   Charlie Carter

SUBSTITUTES: Niall Moloney for John Power; P.J. Delaney for Charlie Carter.

CORK
BACK ROW L TO R: Diarmuid Ó Sullivan, Brian Corcoran, John Browne, Fergal McCormack, Wayne Sherlock, Donal Óg Cusack, Seán Óg Ó h-Ailpín
FRONT ROW L TO R: Seanie McGrath, Mickey O'Connell, Ben O'Connor, Mark Landers, Neil Ronan, Fergal Ryan, Timmy McCarthy, Joe Deane

KILKENNY
BACK ROW L TO R: Philip Larkin, Brian McEvoy, Henry Shefflin, John Power, Andy Comerford, Canice Brennan, Peter Barry, Pat O'Neill
FRONT ROW L TO R: Willie O'Connor, Michael Kavanagh, James McGarry, Denis Byrne, D.J. Carey, Ken O'Shea, Charlie Carter

SATURDAY, MAY 22, 1999

MUNSTER SENIOR HURLING CHAMPIONSHIP

TIPPERARY versus KERRY

SEMPLE STADIUM (THURLES)

REFEREE EAMONN MORRIS (DUBLIN):

RESULT: TIPPERARY 4-29 KERRY 2-6

TIPPERARY'S TWENTY-NINE POINTS WINNING MARGIN says it all! The newly-crowned League Champions completely outclassed a disappointing Kerry side in a game that once again underlined the gulf in class between the stronger counties and those in the lower echelons. To put it mildly, this was a mismatch and soul-destroying for the Kerry hurlers while, at the same time, of little relevance to Tipperary in advance of their clash with Clare in the Munster semi-final. No team deserves to be trounced by twenty-nine points and urgent action is required if a re-occurrence is to be avoided. .

No fewer than nine Tipperary players found the target with Paul Shelly top scoring with 2-2 while Thomas Dunne had scored seven points before being called ashore early in the second half.

All six Tipperary forwards had found the target by the 13th minute of the opening half and even at that early stage it was evident that Kerry were struggling badly in many positions. Thomas Dunne scored the first point of the new hurling season after little more than one minute. It was a sign of things to come when Paul Shelly took a pass from Brian O'Meara and crashed the ball to the net in the 13th minute for the first goal of 'Championship '99. Padraig Cronin gave Kerry some breathing space when he scored a fine goal but very soon afterwards Shelly scored his second when he turned his marker, set off on a solo run and shot to the net. Again, Kerry responded and Brendan O'Sullivan shot high into the roof of the net past Tipperary goalkeeper Brendan Cummins for a superb goal. Kerry goalkeeper, John Healy then tipped a goalbound shot from Declan Ryan over the crossbar. Healy had a fine game between the Kerry posts and the Ballyheigue man thwarted Tipperary on many occasions with timely saves.

The impressive Tony Maunsell and Michael Slattery fired over a point each for Kerry in quick succession but thereafter Tipperary took control and cruised to victory. Despite playing against the breeze, Tipperary held a seven-point advantage, 2-12 to 2-5, at the interval and clearly only the margin of victory remained to be resolved. Near the end of the opening half a rocket-like shot from Declan Ryan came off the crossbar with such force that the thud of the sliothar on the woodwork could he heard around Semple Stadium.

It was a brave first half showing by Kerry against a razor-sharp Tipperary forward line where John Leahy, Paul Shelly and Thomas Dunne led the charge. Leahy, ever the artist, showed some wonderful deft touches to open up the Kerry defence on numerous occasions.

Dunne coverted two frees shortly after the re-start and, with his evening's work complete, was replaced by Paul Kelly, who proceeded to score four points from play. Kerry were reduced to fourteen players nine minutes into the second half when Tom Cronin was sent off for a second bookable offence.

Tipperary outscored Kerry by 2-17 to 0-1 in the second half to illustrate the one-sided nature of the game with Liam Cahill and Declan Ryan, from a penalty in injury-time, scoring the goals. Tipperary's hurling class and know-how was very much in evidence all through and the final whistle was a welcome relief to the Kerry players. Indeed, by the time Dublin referee Eamonn Morris called a halt to proceedings, Tipperary had surged twenty-nine points clear, the biggest winning margin of the hurling Championship. Furthermore, Tipperary's tally of 4-29 was the highest recorded in the '99 Championship.

SCORERS – TIPPERARY: Paul Shelly 2-2; Thomas Dunne 0-7; John Leahy 0-6; Paul Kelly 0-4; Declan Ryan 1-2; Liam Cahill 1-2; Brian O'Meara 0-3; Conor Gleeson 0-2; Eddie Enright 0-1.
KERRY: Michael Slattery 0-3; Tony Maunsell 0-3; Padraig Cronin 1-0; Brendan O'Sullivan 1-0

TIPPERARY

Brendan Cummins

| Donnacha Fahy | Fergal Heaney | Liam Sheedy |
| Conal Bonnar | David Kennedy | Eamonn Corcoran |

Declan Carr   Eddie Enright

| Thomas Dunne (Captain) | Declan Ryan | Brian O'Meara |
| Liam Cahill | Paul Shelly | John Leahy |

SUBSTITUTES: Paul Kelly for Thomas Dunne; George Frend for Conal Bonnar;
Conor Gleeson for Declan Carr

KERRY

John Healy

| Tom Cronin | Seamus McIntyre | Ian Brick |
| David Slattery | Maurice McCarthy | Willie Joe Leen |

Brendan O'Sullivan   Pat Cronin

| Padraig Cronin | Christy Walsh | Michael Slattery |
| Tony Maunsell | John Joe Canty (Captain) | T.P. O'Connor |

SUBSTITUTES: Michael Hanafin for David Slattery; Michael O'Regan for Seamus McIntyre;
Ian Maunsell for T.P. O'Connor

TIPPERARY
BACK ROW L TO R: Liam Sheedy, Brian O'Meara, Fergal Heaney, Brendan Cummins, Eddie Enright, Declan Carr, Eamonn Corcoran, Conal Bonnar
FRONT ROW L TO R: Declan Ryan, Donnacha Fahy, Paul Shelly, Thomas Dunne, John Leahy, David Kennedy, Liam Cahill.

KERRY
BACK ROW L TO R: Brendan O'Sullivan, Pat Cronin, Seamus McIntyre, Maurice McCarthy, John Healy, Christy Walsh, Tony Maunsell, T. P. O'Connor, Ian Brick
FRONT ROW L TO R: David Slattery, Tom Cronin, Michael Slattery, John Joe Canty, Padraig Cronin, Willie Joe Leen

SUNDAY, MAY 30, 1999

MUNSTER SENIOR HURLING CHAMPIONSHIP QUARTER-FINAL

LIMERICK versus WATERFORD

PÁIRC UÍ CHAOIMH

REFEREE: PAT HORAN (OFFALY)

RESULT: WATEFORD 1-16 LIMERICK 1-15

WATERFORD HAD TO CALL ON ALL THEIR RESILIENCE to survive a late onslaught from Limerick before eventually qualifying to meet Cork in the Munster semi-final. Brave Limerick, one of the unlucky teams of the nineties after All-Ireland defeats in '94 and '96, did remarkably well to recover from a dismal opening twenty minutes, to push the Decies men to the limit in an absorbing second half. Waterford displayed tremendous character in a pulsating final quarter which saw Limerick attack incessantly in a desperate attempt to keep their Championship hopes alive. Waterford wing-back Brian Greene was dismissed in the 49th minute for a second bookable offence and crucially Limerick made good use of the extra player, Ciarán Carey, as their bold bid for victory gained momentum.

Limerick scored 1-7 in the closing twenty minutes, as the excitement among their supporters reached fever pitch in the expectation of a winning comeback. But Waterford continued to hold their nerve and Paul Flynn and Ken McGrath hit over vital points to keep the Limerick men at bay. The joy among players, supporters and officials at the finish showed just what this victory meant to Waterford.

The game began at a frantic pace and Waterford goalkeeper Brendan Landers was called on to make a save early on. There was nothing spared in the early exchanges as both teams endeavoured to gain the upperhand. After a bright opening few minutes, during which Barry Foley fired over the first point of the game, Limerick lost their way as Waterford powered ahead with a point each from Ken McGrath, Paul Flynn and Dave Bennett.

Two further points from Flynn and one from McGrath pushed Waterford into a commanding 0-6 to 0-1 lead by the 16th minute. Limerick, who missed a number of good scoring opportunities in the opening quarter, were dealt a severe body blow when Flynn scored a superb goal after racing in from the right wing. Manager Eamonn Cregan re-arranged his forward line in an effort to revive the Limerick challenge. Mike Galligan pointed three frees in as many minutes to stem the tide as Limerick's play gradually improved in the latter stages of the first half. Waterford led at the interval by 1-9 to 0-7 with Paul Flynn scoring 1-4 of that total.

Within two minutes of the re-start, Waterford goalkeeper Brendan Landers brought off a superb save to deprive Mike Galligan a certain goal. It was a vital save! Waterford had increased their lead to six points by the time Brian Greene received his marching orders for a heavy challenge on Ciarán Carey.

Even though Paul Flynn landed two points and Micheál White found the target for the second time, Limerick slowly but surely began to put 14-man Waterford under pressure. Mike Houlihan finished a long ball from Dave Clarke to the Waterford net and suddenly Limerick had thundered back into the game. Clem Smith further helped their cause with a fine point but that was cancelled out with a superb point from play by the excellent Ken McGrath, his fourth of the match. Waterford had a lucky escape when Mike Houlihan's rocket-like shot skimmed narrowly wide in the 61st minute. Mark Foley and substitute Gary Kirby both scored a point each as Limerick fought back in determined fashion. Supporters braced themselves for a grandstand finish when Gary Kirby converted his fourth free to move within a point of Waterford with three minutes remaining. It was nail biting stuff and not for the faint-hearted. Top scorer Paul Flynn brought his tally to 1-8 with a point from a free to ease the pressure on Waterford but Limerick had the final say when Dave Clarke fired over a point right on time after taking a short free from Gary Kirby. Shortly afterwards, Offaly referee Pat Horan called a halt to proceedings and as Waterford players and supporters alike celebrated, Limerick were left to reflect on what might have been were it not for some wayward shooting in the opening half. But Waterford deserved their victory on a day when the character of the team was tested to the full and the players proved their pedigree and responded to the challenge with gusto.

Paul Flynn proved himself to be a player of the highest quality and his point from play in the 46th minute was nothing short of pure magic. Ken McGrath turned in a highly impressive performance while Peter Queally and Seán Cullinane were other star performers for the Decies men.

Miracle-man Tony Browne, more than any other player, typified the spirit of the Waterford team by lining out against the odds from the start, despite suffering from a very painful ankle injury. The 1998 All-Star 'Hurler of the Year' had been effectively ruled out of the game midweek after severely damaging ankle ligaments at a training session in Fraher Field just a week before the game.

SCORERS – WATERFORD: Paul Flynn 1-8; Ken McGrath 0-4; Micheál White 0-2; Dave Bennett 0-1; Fergal Hartley 0-1
LIMERICK: Gary Kirby 0-4; Mike Galligan 0-3; Mike Houlihan 1-0; Barry Foley 0-2; James Moran 0-2; Dave Clarke 0-1; Clem Smith 0-1; Mark Foley 0-1; Ciarán Carey 0-1

WATERFORD

Brendan Landers

Tom Feeney   Seán Cullinane   Brian Flannery (Captain)

Peter Queally   Stephen Frampton   Brian Greene

Fergal Hartley   Tony Browne

Dan Shanahan   Billy O'Sullivan   Ken McGrath

Micheál White   Paul Flynn   Dave Bennett

SUBSTITUTES: Anthony Kirwan for Dave Bennett; Barry Browne for Micheál White

LIMERICK

Joe Quaid

Stephen McDonagh   Brian Begley   Brian Geary

Dave Clarke   Ollie Moran (Captain)   Clem Smith

Ciarán Carey   Jack Foley

James Moran   Mike Houlihan   Barry Foley

Mark Foley   Shane O'Neill   Mike Galligan

SUBSTITUTES: Gary Kirby for Mike Galligan; T.J. Ryan for Shane O'Neill;
Declan Nash for James Moran

WATERFORD
BACK ROW L TO R: Paul Flynn, Brían Greene, Dave Bennett, Micheál White, Fergal Hartley, Ken McGrath, Brendan Landers, Dan Shanahan
FRONT ROW L TO R: Peter Queally, Seán Cullinane, Stephen Frampton, Tony Browne, Billy O'Sullivan, Brian Flannery, Tom Feeney

LIMERICK
BACK ROW L TO R: Mike Houlihan, Barry Foley, Brian Geary, Shane O'Neill, Joe Quaid, Brian Begley, Clem Smith, Dave Clarke
FRONT ROW L TO R: Stephen McDonagh, Ollie Moran, John Foley, Ciarán Carey, Mike Galligan, James Moran, Mark Foley

SUNDAY, JUNE 6, 1999

MUNSTER SENIOR HURLING CHAMPIONSHIP SEMI-FINAL

CLARE versus TIPPERARY

PÁIRC UÍ CHAOIMH (CORK)

REFEREE: DICKIE MURPHY (WEXFORD)

RESULT: CLARE 2-12 TIPPERARY 0-18 (A DRAW)

MEMORIES ARE MADE OF THIS! Mighty goalkeeper Davy Fitzgerald saved Clare's Championship season by scoring a dramatic injury-time goal from a penalty to spark off incredible scenes of jubilation among the Banner faithful. As the game entered the final minute, substitute Conor Clancy was grounded by Fergal Heaney and referee Dickie Murphy awarded a penalty. All eyes turned to Davy and there was tension in the air as he made his way towards the Tipp goal. The pocket rocket from Sixmilebridge displayed nerves of steel, under enormous pressure, as he drove the ball low and hard. Goalkeeper Brendan Cummins, who was rock solid all afternoon, along with defenders Fergal Heaney and Liam Sheedy could only watch on in despair as the sliothar ended up in the corner of the net.

Cummins made a brave effort to block the shot but was unable to prevent his Clare counterpart scoring a 'golden goal' that kept Clare's Championship hopes alive.

Earlier, Fitzgerald had pulled off a number of vital saves to keep Clare in the game including one particularly breathtaking save to deprive Paul Shelly of a certain goal that would surely have sealed Clare's fate.

This was a game Tipperary should have won but credit Clare for persevering to the very end and forcing a draw against the odds. The hurling was fast and furious from the start, but despite the intensity of the exchanges, referee Dickie Murphy had no reason to brandish even one yellow card.

There were many highlights in this absorbing Munster semi-final that gave new meaning to determination, commitment and passion. The Tipperary defence was outstanding all through, none more so than centre-half-back David Kennedy who reigned supreme. Paul Shelly and Liam Cahill proved more than a handful for the much-vaunted Clare defence while all around the field Tipperary players won many of the personal clashes. As for Clare: Liam Doyle was superb in defence; Jamesie O'Connor scored his first goal in Championship hurling; Colin Lynch played his part at midfield; Conor Clancy made a very significant contribution when introduced by scoring a point and winning a penalty while Fitzgerald was outstanding all through. His equalising goal capped a magnificent individual display.

The sides were level on no fewer than six occasions in the course of a thundering first half during which there were many text-book scores, including the opening point of the game from David Forde. Thomas Dunne levelled the match in the 5th minute and then edged his team ahead for the first time with a point from a '65. Over the next five minutes, Clare hit over three unanswered points – all from play – one each from Seán McMahon, Colin Lynch and Barry Murphy but Tipperary were back on level terms for the third time by the 12th minute through points from Liam Cahill and John Leahy. The Tipperary tactic of pucking the ball out ultra-quickly often unsettled the Clare backs and good scores accrued, particularly so a splendid point from Liam Cahill in the 20th minute. The Clare full forward line found it extremely difficult to break down a resolute Tipperary defence.

Thomas Dunne's fourth point in the 32nd minute left Tipperary narrowly ahead 0-8 to 0-7 at half-time, a favourable position considering the fact that Clare would have to face the breeze in the second half. There was certainly some significant activity in the opening five minutes of the second half.

Jamesie O'Connor missed a free; Brian O'Meara whipped over a point from play; Paul Shelly got past Brian Lohan and struck the ball over the bar while Ollie Baker, who failed to start because of injury, came in at full forward for Clare in place of Stephen McNamara. It was five minutes of hard, tough hurling that saw Tipperary move three points clear but that lead was cancelled out when Niall Gilligan delivered a pass to Jamesie O'Connor, who rifled the ball to the net for the equalising score.

It was Jamesie's first Championship goal! David Forde then scored a point to put Clare 1-8 to 0-10 ahead by the 45th minute as the game once again gathered pace with Tipperary leading the charge. Tipp outscored Clare by 0-5 to 0-1 from the 45th to the 59th minute to surge 0-15 to 1-9 clear.

Once again spirited Clare, although not moving with the fluency of other days, displayed tremendous character to claw their way back through points from David Forde, Niall Gilligan and substitute Conor Clancy to reduce the margin to the minimum. Davy Fitzgerald then brought off a wonder save from Paul Shelly at the expense of a '65, which was converted by Thomas Dunne. Shelly added another point and Tipperary appeared to be on their way to victory until Davy Fitzgerald scored that last-gasp equalising goal from a penalty. Interestingly, nine players from each side scored on what was a day of high emotion at Páirc Uí Chaoimh.

SCORERS – CLARE: Jamesie O'Connor 1-2; David Forde 0-3; Davy Fitzgerald 1-0;
Niall Gilligan 0-2; Seán McMahon 0-1; Barry Murphy 0-1; Colin Lynch 0-1; Alan Markham 0-1;
Conor Clancy 0-1
TIPPERARY: Thomas Dunne 0-7; Liam Cahill 0-3; Paul Shelly 0-2; John Leahy 0-1;
Eddie Enright 0-1; Brian O'Meara 0-1; Eddie Tucker 0-1; Declan Ryan 0-1; Paul Kelly 0-1

CLARE

Davy Fitzgerald

| Brian Quinn | Brian Lohan | Frank Lohan |
| Liam Doyle | Seán McMahon | Anthony Daly (Captain) |

Enda Flannery   Colin Lynch

| Jamesie O'Connor | Niall Gilligan | Alan Markham |
| David Forde | Stephen McNamara | Barry Murphy |

SUBSTITUTES: Ollie Baker for Stephen McNamara; Conor Clancy for Alan Markham

---

TIPPERARY

Brendan Cummins

| Donnacha Fahy | Fergal Heaney | Liam Sheedy |
| Conal Bonnar | David Kennedy | Eamonn Corcoran |

Eddie Enright   Conor Gleeson

| Thomas Dunne (Captain) | Declan Ryan | Brian O'Meara |
| Liam Cahill | Paul Shelly | John Leahy |

SUBSTITUTES: Paul Kelly for Brian O'Meara; Eddie Tucker for John Leahy

CLARE
BACK ROW L TO R: Brian Lohan, Colin Lynch, Frank Lohan, Enda Flannery, Davy Fitzgerald, Niall Gilligan, Alan Markham, Barry Murphy, Seán McMahon
FRONT ROW L TO R: Liam Doyle, David Forde, Anthony Daly, Jamesie O'Connor, Brian Quinn, Stephen McNamara

TIPPERARY
BACK ROW L TO R: John Leahy, Donnacha Fahy, Brian O'Meara, Brendan Cummins, Conor Gleeson, Eddie Enright, Liam Sheedy, Declan Ryan
FRONT ROW L TO R: Fergal Heaney, Paul Shelly, Eamonn Corcoran, Thomas Dunne, Conal Bonnar, David Kennedy, Liam Cahill

SATURDAY, JUNE 12, 1999

MUNSTER SENIOR HURLING CHAMPIONSHIP SEMI-FINAL (REPLAY)

CLARE versus TIPPERARY

PÁIRC UÍ CHAOIMH, CORK

REFEREE: DICKIE MURPHY (WEXFORD)

RESULT: CLARE 1-21 TIPPERARY 1-11

FEW PEOPLE LEAVING THE VENUE SIX DAYS EARLIER could have anticipated such an outcome! Clare pride had been hurt and it was time to restore self-respect. And, how magnificently they responded. Tipperary were but a pale shadow of the team which had thrilled supporters in the first game. There was never a stage when they could have been considered to be in serious contention for a win. Clare manager Ger Loughnane said afterwards that it was arguably the team's 'most perfect' display in the five years he had been in charge.

Everything about Clare on the day was calculated to produce the desired result. People who saw them enter the ground remarked on how 'focused' they were on their way to the dressingroom. The same type of approach manifested itself in their play from the opening minutes. Tactically and in every other respect, Clare were about to impose their will on the game to an extent that must have shocked even the Tipperary management. Little or nothing was to go right for Tipp on the day. As early as the 9th minute, Clare were six points clear 1-4 to 0-1. The goal had come from Alan Markham, from an opening created by Barry Murphy.

Everything went according to plan for the Clare management. Firstly, the team established a strong grip in defence – where the outstanding play of Brian and Frank Lohan ensured that neither Paul Shelly nor Liam Cahill would exert the type of influence they did the first day. Then, Clare assumed a steady dominance of midfield. Thirdly, the adoption of a well-prepared forward strategy was hugely successful.

In the drawn match, young centre-back David Kennedy had been one of Tipperary's stars. This time he struggled to get into the game, faced by a very determined Enda Flannery. Additionally, Jamesie O'Connor – placed at left corner-forward at the throw-in – effectively operated as an outfield player, which allowed Barry Murphy and Niall Gilligan plenty of room. The result was that the forwards conjured up some marvellous scores.

Midfield was crucial in the sense that Ollie Baker's match fitness gave the team a massive boost. And, in turn, his support allowed Colin Lynch the freedom to play his normal game. It earned him four points from play and was, popularly, the team's outstanding player. Half-time arrived with Clare enjoying a comfortable lead of seven points, 1-12 to 0-8.

The only negative feature was that Jamesie O'Connor had to go off injured five minutes before the interval. Jamesie received a serious hand injury, which subsequently needed surgery to have a plate inserted, and, while his departure was a blow to the team, it failed to restrict the attack..

Tipperary were over-dependant on the accuracy from frees of team captain Thomas Dunne, who was to score ten points. Declan Ryan, surprisingly omitted, was introduced to the attack late in the first half and got their only goal from a free in the 56th minute. It was to be their last score of the game, even though Ryan went close to getting another goal from a later free.

SCORERS - CLARE: Alan Markham 1-3; Seán McMahon 0-5; Colin Lynch 0-4; Barry Murphy 0-3; David Forde 0-2; Jamesie O'Connor 0-1; Anthony Daly 0-1; Ollie Baker 0-1; Enda Flannery 0-1. TIPPERARY – Thomas Dunne 0-10; Declan Ryan 1-0; Eddie Enright 0-1.

CLARE

Davy Fitzgerald

Brian Quinn	Brian Lohan	Frank Lohan
Liam Doyle	Seán McMahon	Anthony Daly (Captain)

Ollie Baker   Colin Lynch

David Forde	Enda Flannery	Alan Markham
Niall Gilligan	Barry Murphy	Jamesie O'Connor

SUBSTITUTES: Conor Clancy for Jamesie O'Connor; P.J. O'Connell for Conor Clancy; Ronan O'Hara for P.J. O'Connell

---

TIPPERARY

Brendan Cummins

Donnacha Fahy	Fergal Heaney	Liam Sheedy
Conal Bonnar	David Kennedy	Eamonn Corcoran

Eddie Enright   Conor Gleeson

Thomas Dunne (Captain)	Eddie Tucker	Brian O'Meara
Liam Cahill	Paul Shelly	John Leahy

SUBSTITUTES: Paul Ormond for Eddie Enright; Declan Ryan for Brian O'Meara; Brian Horgan for Conal Bonnar

CLARE
BACK ROW L TO R: Brian Lohan, Colin Lynch, Enda Flannery, Frank Lohan, Davy Fitzgerald, Alan Markham, Barry Murphy, Seán McMahon
FRONT ROW L TO R: Liam Doyle, David Forde, Ollie Baker, Anthony Daly, Jamesie O'Connor, Brian Quinn, Niall Gilligan

TIPPERARY
BACK ROW L TO R: John Leahy, Paul Shelly, Brian O'Meara, Brendan Cummins, Conor Gleeson, Eddie Enright, Eddie Tucker, Liam Sheedy
FRONT ROW L TO R: Donnacha Fahy, Fergal Heaney, Eamonn Corcoran, Thomas Dunne, Conal Bonnar, David Kennedy, Liam Cahill

SUNDAY, JUNE 13, 1999

MUNSTER SENIOR HURLING CHAMPIONSHIP SEMI-FINAL

CORK versus WATERFORD

SEMPLE STADIUM, THURLES

REFEREE: AODHAN MacSUIBHNE (DUBLIN)

RESULT: CORK 0-24 WATERFORD 1-15

IT WAS THE DAY OF RECKONING for Jimmy Barry-Murphy, the day that would decide his team's immediate future and, to all intents and purposes, his fate as a manager. The fact that the opposition was provided by neighbours Waterford and that they were coached by Barry-Murphy's former St. Finbarrs and Cork team-mate Gerald McCarthy added to the attraction of the game.

In advance of the game, Cork supporters and, indeed, the hurling public at large, reacted with a mixture of surprise and intrigue to the announcement of the team. It featured six players new to championship hurling although all of them had featured on the All-Ireland winning Under-21 teams of the previous two seasons.

Waterford had every reason to feel confident about the outcome, because of their greater experience gained from their two appearances in Croke Park the previous summer. However, there were concerns about the match fitness of Tony Browne, troubled by a recurring ankle problem. Cork began the game confidently, boosted by their strength in defence – with Brian Corcoran, typically, quick to assert his authority. It was to prove all the more important because, behind him Paul Flynn was a big threat in the full forward line. As the game developed, it was Cork's control around the midfield area, which was to prove crucial. It stemmed mainly from the dominance of Midleton's Mickey O'Connell – one of the newcomers – who was to give an exhibition of point-scoring – from play and frees. And, he was to be strongly supported by team captain Mark Landers, a regular at wing-back on the team which won the League title.

Scores were to be level four times up to the 21st minute, at which stage Cork took the lead for the first time. The scorer was Ben O'Connor – another newcomer! In general, both attacks were finding it difficult to get scores, but it was Cork who had the greater amount of chances – and it was the principal reason why they turned over at half-time with a three-point lead, 0-10 to 0-7.

Waterford, taking confidence from an improvement in the half-forward line, hit over two quick scores on the resumption and Cork came under pressure for the first of several times in the half.

However, they showed commendable character – benefiting from the leadership of Joe

Deane at full-forward - when responding each time to Waterford scores. And, the team was to be greatly encouraged by the improvement achieved by Diarmuid O'Sullivan against Paul Flynn. Likewise, his Cloyne club-mate Donal Óg Cusack was totally dependable in his first Championship game in goal. Mickey O'Connell continued to impress. Substitute Billy O'Sullivan and Ken McGrath were hurling well for Waterford while Peter Queally at right half-back was maintaining the high standard he set early in the game.

Cork hopes rose as Timmy McCarthy picked off some great scores. Waterford were still very much in contention when Paul Flynn goaled from a free in the 56th minute to leave them only two points behind. It looked anybody's game, but Cork seemed to move up a gear and picked off a series of scores to finally kill off the Waterford challenge.

At the final whistle, Jimmy Barry-Murphy sprinted on to the field to embrace his players. It was a rare show of emotion from him – reflecting the enormous relief he experienced at the final whistle.

SCORERS: CORK – Mickey O'Connell 0-8; Joe Deane 0-7; Timmy McCarthy 0-3;
Mark Landers 0-2; Brian Corcoran 0-1; Fergal McCormack 0-1; Ben O'Connor 0-1; Kevin Murray 0-1.
WATERFORD – Paul Flynn 1-4; Ken McGrath 0-4; Dan Shanahan 0-3; Dave Bennett 0-1;
Micheál White 0-1; Stephen Frampton 0-1; Michael Molumphy 0-1.

CORK

Donal Óg Cusack

Fergal Ryan | Diarmuid O'Sullivan | John Browne

Wayne Sherlock | Brian Corcoran | Seán Óg Ó hAilpín

Mark Landers (Captain) | Mickey O'Connell

Timmy McCarthy | Fergal McCormack | Seanie McGrath

Ben O'Connor | Joe Deane | Neil Ronan

SUBSTITUTES: Kevin Murray for Ben O'Connor; Alan Browne for Seanie McGrath

---

WATERFORD

Brendan Landers

Tom Feeney | Seán Cullinane Brian Flannery (Captain)

Peter Queally | Stephen Frampton | Brian Greene

Tony Browne | Fergal Hartley

Dan Shanahan | Billy O'Sullivan | Ken McGrath

Micheál White | Paul Flynn | Dave Bennett

SUBSTITUTES: Pat Walsh for Fergal Hartley; Anthony Kirwan for Brian Greene;
Michael Molumphy for Dave Bennett

CORK
BACK ROW L TO R: Diarmuid O' Sullivan, Brian Corcoran, John Browne, Donal Óg Cusack, Fergal McCormack, Wayne Sherlock, Seán Óg Ó hAilpín
FRONT ROW L TO R: Mickey O'Connell, Ben O'Connor, Seanie McGrath, Mark Landers, Neil Ronan, Fergal Ryan, Joe Deane, Timmy McCarthy

WATERFORD
BACK ROW L TO R: Paul Flynn, Brian Greene, Fergal Hartley, Ken McGrath, Brendan Landers, Dan Shanahan, Peter Queally
FRONT ROW L TO R: Tony Browne, Seán Cullinane, Billy O'Sullivan, Micheál White, Dave Bennett, Brian Flannery, Stephen Frampton, Tom Feeney

SUNDAY, JULY 4, 1999

MUNSTER SENIOR HURLING CHAMPIONSHIP FINAL

CORK versus CLARE

SEMPLE STADIUM THURLES

REFEREE: DICKIE MURPHY (WEXFORD)

RESULT: CORK 1-15 CLARE 0-14

JUBILANT JIMMY BARRY-MURPHY aptly summed it up! "It's been a long four years, but well worth the wait," he said after Cork had achieved a remarkable victory over the holders. A number of factors were to prove crucial, none more so, perhaps, than a disputed goal scored by Joe Deane two minutes before the interval. Coupled with an unexpected let-off, when David Forde inexplicably missed a 20 metres free near the end which would have levelled the scores, it propelled the young Cork side to the county's first provincial title in seven years.

Without question, Cork benefited from their recent championship encounters with Clare, especially from the 1998 meeting when Ger Loughnane's team proved stronger. This time they were fresher, having taken a more relaxed approach to the League. And, they better prepared mentally.

Starting without Jamesie O'Connor, ruled out as a result of the injury he received in the replay against Tipperary, it was noteworthy that Clare struggled quite a lot in the opening stages of the game – despite the fact that they were backed by the wind. They were making little progress in attack largely as a consequence of the excellent work of the Cork backs. Amazingly, they were never to take the lead at any stage.

Cork were always very comfortable at the back, with Blackrock club-mates Wayne Sherlock and Fergal Ryan forming a formidable right flank. Brian Corcoran – the only link with the successful 1992 side – was dominant in the centre and, with Seán Óg Ó hAilpín playing his part on the other side, Cork's half line was almost impenetrable at times. Midfield exchanges were fairly even for a lot of the time, with the comparatively inexperienced Cork pairing of team captain Mark Landers and Mickey O'Connell doing well against Ollie Baker and Colin Lynch. Worrying from a Clare point of view was the fact that Baker twice had to receive treatment on the field for an ankle injury, which was eventually to force him off. Up front, Cork were making progress on a fairly continuous basis, except that they were dogged by some bad finishing.

Scores were level at 0-3 each after eleven minutes before Cork again opened up a three points gap by the 26th minute. And, the margin was down to a single point nearing the break. That was because of the combination of Cork's wastage of good possession and the failure of the Clare forwards to make an impact. It highlighted the loss of Jamesie

O'Connor.

Then a stroke of genius from Seanie McGrath produced a magical goal for Joe Deane. A long ball from Fergal McCormack appeared to be going wide until McGrath, literally with a flick of the wrist, brought it back into play. Deane connected with the ball and it flew into the net.

The Clare backs protested that Deane had been inside the square but the score stood and Cork, boosted by two late points, went to their dressingroom in high spirits leading by six points, 1-10 to 0-7.

In a matter of three minutes that lead had been halved, with Baker contributing two of the points. Predictably, it inspired Clare and, for a period, they threatened a take-over with Frank Lohan and Liam Doyle in fine form. Equally, Niall Gilligan began to make an important contribution after moving to centre-forward which meant that Cork began to struggle.

Nevertheless, the Cork backs continued to play their part, with Diarmuid O'Sullivan inspirational at full-back. Baker was forced off injured in the 50th minute, while Cork were to benefit from the introduction of Alan Browne at left half-forward. Yet, with Cork again missing good scoring chances, the game was very much in the balance until David Forde hit a 20 metre free wide three minutes from the end.

That was the break that Cork needed. Deane hit over two points from frees and young Ben O'Connor scored a fabulous point in injury time. Nothing was going to stop Cork from winning at that stage.

SCORERS – CORK: Joe Deane 1-4; Mickey O'Connell 0-5; Ben O'Connor 0-2; Seanie McGrath 0-2; Neil Ronan 0-1; Fergal McCormack 0-1.
CLARE: Niall Gilligan 0-3; David Forde 0-3; Ollie Baker 0-2; Ronan O'Hara 0-1; Seán McMahon 0-1. Alan Markham 0-1; Barry Murphy 0-1; Colin Lynch 0-1; Danny Scanlan 0-1.

CORK

Donal Óg Cusack

Fergal Ryan   Diarmuid O'Sullivan   John Browne

Wayne Sherlock   Brian Corcoran   Seán Óg Ó hAilpín

Mickey O'Connell   Mark Landers (Captain)

Timmy McCarthy   Fergal McCormack   Neil Ronan

Seanie McGrath   Joe Deane   Ben O'Connor

SUBSTITUTES: Pat Ryan for Mark Landers; Alan Browne for Neil Ronan; Kevin Murray for Seanie McGrath.

CORK
BACK ROW L TO R: Diarmuid O' Sullivan, Brian Corcoran, John Browne, Fergal McCormack, Wayne Sherlock,
Donal Óg Cusack, Seán Óg Ó hAilpín
FRONT ROW L TO R: Seanie McGrath, Mickey O'Connell, Fergal Ryan, Ben O'Connor, Mark Landers, Neil Ronan,
Timmy McCarthy, Joe Deane.

CLARE
BACK ROW L TO R: Brian Lohan, Colin Lynch, Frank Lohan, Enda Flannery, Ronan O'Hara, Davy Fitzgerald, Alan Markham,
Barry Murphy, Seán McMahon
FRONT ROW L TO R: Liam Doyle, David Forde, Ollie Baker, Anthony Daly, Jamesie O'Connor, Brian Quinn, Niall Gilligan

WEXFORD versus DUBLIN

NOWLAN PARK (KILKENNY)
REFEREE: PAT O'CONNOR (LIMERICK)
RESULT: WEXFORD 1-13 DUBLIN 1-12

DUBLIN CAME AGONISINGLY CLOSE TO PULLING OFF the first big shock of the 1999 hurling Championship when a magnificent late rally yielded 1-5 against a shell-shocked Wexford side that had led by nine points with little more than ten minutes remaining. It was a remarkable fightback for Dublin! Wexford, who lost out to Offaly through a late, late Johnny Dooley goal in last year's Championship, were forced to hold on for dear life at the finish and were mightily relieved when Pat O'Connor blew the full-time whistle. Dublin had sixteen wides against nine for a Wexford team that took the foot off the pedal in the third quarter and very nearly paid the ultimate price. Wexford had a very lucky escape as everyone involved with the team that I spoke with afterwards freely admitted. The Dubs outscored Wexford by 1-8 to 0-4 in the course of a hugely entertaining, high-tension second half that had the crowd on tenterhooks particularly in the closing tension-filled minutes.

Wexford powered their way to an eight-point half-time lead, 1-9 to 0-4, thanks mainly to superb displays from Adrian Fenlon and Larry O'Gorman, two of the heroes of the '96 All-Ireland winning side. O'Gorman played superbly at wing-back while 'Man of the Match', Fenlon produced a stunning display of all that is positive in the game. The Rapparees player scored five points in the first half – four from play and one from a side-line cut – as Wexford availed of most of the scoring chances that came their way in total contrast to Dublin.

Liam Walsh fired over the opening point for Dublin, but by the time Tomás McGrane got their second point some seventeen minutes later, Wexford had built up a sizeable lead. Michael 'Mitch' Jordan took a pass from the impressive Larry Murphy and rifled the ball past Dublin goalkeeper Brendan McLoughlin after nine minutes play.

Wexford continued to pick off scores to move further and further ahead as Dublin's wides began to mount up. Conor McCann missed a glorious chance of a goal when he shot too hastily and the ball went wide. Darragh Ryan was playing superbly at centre-half-forward and his loss to Wexford was immeasurable after he retired injured at the interval. Wexford won many of the man to man duels in the opening half and it was difficult to visualise how Dublin could possibly peg back an eight points half-time deficit. But, as it happened, Wexford's second half showing bore hardly any resemblance to what had transpired before the break.

Favoured by the breeze, Dublin had reduced the margin to six points within thirteen minutes of the re-start with a point each from David Sweeney, Conor McCann and Michael Fitzsimons in reply to a Wexford point from their captain Paul Codd. Then Martin Storey burst into action and scored two points from play and when Codd tacked on his third of the afternoon Wexford appeared to have done more than enough to secure a Leinster semi-final clash with All-Ireland Champions Offaly.

No one took too much notice when David Sweeney and Tomás McGrane scored a point each for Dublin to close the gap marginally. Suddenly, the game changed dramatically as the Dubs exposed deficiencies in the Wexford defence. And all the while Liam Walsh continued to produce high-quality hurling at wing-back for the Dubs. Niall Butler and Tomás McGrane scored a point apiece and Wexford's hearts missed a beat when Emmett Carroll crashed the ball to the net. Michael O'Grady's astute substitutions certainly helped turn the tide. By now it was evident that everything Dublin touched turned to gold. Kevin Flynn cut the deficit to the minimum with a point from play but dual player Shane Ryan was unlucky to see his effort for the equalising point sail narrowly wide of the posts. Another hard luck story for Dublin and a let-off for Wexford. There were lessons to be learned for both sides but only Wexford can now put them into practice.

SCORERS – WEXFORD: Adrian Fenlon 0-5; Michael 'Mitch' Jordan 1-1; Paul Codd 0-3;
Tom Dempsey 0-2; Martin Storey 0-2
DUBLIN: Tomás McGrane 0-5; Emmett Carroll 1-0; David Sweeney 0-2;
Liam Walsh 0-1; Conor McCann 0-1; Michael Fitzsimons 0-1; Niall Butler 0-1; Kevin Flynn 0-1

WEXFORD

Damien Fitzhenry

Colm Kehoe	Ger Cushe	Seán Flood
Declan Ruth	Liam Dunne	Larry O'Gorman

	Adrian Fenlon	Rory McCarthy	

Larry Murphy	Darragh Ryan	Paul Codd (Captain)
Tom Dempsey	Martin Storey	Michael 'Mitch' Jordan

SUBSTITUTES: Eamonn Scallan for Darragh Ryan

DUBLIN

Brendan McLoughlin

John Finnegan   Seán Power (Captain)   Seán Duignan

Liam Walsh   Barry O'Sullivan   David McLoughlin

Michael Fitzsimons   David Sweeney

Shane Martin   Liam Ryan   Shane Ryan

Tomás McGrane   Conor McCann   Kevin Flynn

SUBSTITUTES: Emmett Carroll for Shane Martin; Darragh Spain for Michael Fitzsimons;
Niall Butler for Conor McCann

WEXFORD
BACK ROW L TO R: Ger Cushe, Martin Storey, Declan Ruth, Darragh Ryan, Larry Murphy, Adrian Fenlon, Larry O'Gorman
FRONT ROW L TO R: Liam Dunne, Colm Kehoe, Damien Fitzhenry, Seán Flood, Tom Dempsey, Paul Codd, Michael Jordan,
Rory McCarthy

DUBLIN
BACK ROW L TO R: John Finnegan, David Sweeney, Liam Ryan, Conor McCann, Barry O'Sullivan, Michael Fitzsimons, Tomás
McGrane, Seán Duignan
FRONT ROW L TO R: David McLoughlin, Brendan McLoughlin, Seán Power, Shane Ryan, Kevin Flynn, Liam Walsh,
Shane Martin

SUNDAY, 20 JUNE, 1999

LEINSTER SENIOR HURLING CHAMPIONSHIP SEMI-FINAL

KILKENNY versus LAOIS

CROKE PARK

REFEREE: MICHAEL WADDING (WATERFORD)

RESULT: KILKENNY 6-21 LAOIS 1-14

HOPE SPRINGS ETERNAL, it is often said. Certainly that would have been the case with the Laois hurlers, when they squared up to Kilkenny, buoyed up by the memory of their meeting twelve months earlier at the same venue. That day, Kilkenny needed all their traditional fighting qualities to salvage a win by three points. Imagine how manager Padraig Horan and the Laois supporters felt as they saw the drama unfold before their eyes this time.

It was dramatic only in the sense that Kilkenny stormed into an early lead and had the game won long before half-time, when they led by 5-12 to 0-4. After a mere twenty minutes – following goals from Andy Comerford, John Power and then D.J. Carey - the writing was on the wall. Kilkenny were in such devastating form that Laois, down thirteen points at that stage, had been set an impossible task. And, so it proved.

Laois were struggling all over the field, despite the best efforts of players like P.J. Peacock in defence and, of course, Niall Rigney. He had been chosen at right half-back but lined out at centre-forward. He was to end up scoring six points from frees, two more from play and the team's only goal. But, it merely had the effect of putting a respectable look on the scoreline at the finish.

The opening Kilkenny goal, which came all the way from Comerford's sideline puck from far out, was crucial. John Power, starting his first championship game in two years, gave the Kilkenny attack added strength and D.J. Carey was in sparkling form as was Ken O'Shea. The opening goal certainly had an element of luck about it, but all the others in the first half were the result of good team play.

Laois, to their credit, battled all the way to the finish. However, their position was further undermined when they had to play most of the second half down a man – after Cyril Cuddy was sent off for a second bookable offence. And, the game was nearing its finality when Niall Rigney scored a fine goal.

SCORERS: KILKENNY – Henry Shefflin 0-10; D.J. Carey 2-3; Ken O'Shea 2-1; John Power 1-1; Andy Comerford 1-0; Charlie Carter 0-3; Brian McEvoy 0-2; Michael Kavanagh 0-1.
LAOIS – Niall Rigney 1-8; Fionán O'Sullivan 0-2; David Cuddy 0-1; John Shortall 0-1; Eamonn Fennelly 0-1; Declan Conroy 0-1.

KILKENNY

James McGarry

Tom Hickey   Canice Brennan   Willie O'Connor

Michael Kavanagh   Eamonn Kennedy   Peter Barry

Denis Byrne (Captain)   Andy Comerford

DJ Carey   John Power   Brian McEvoy

Ken O'Shea   Henry Shefflin   Charlie Carter

SUBSTITUTES: John Costello for Eamonn Kennedy; PJ Delaney for Brian McEvoy; Niall Moloney for DJ Carey

LAOIS

Ricky Cashin

PJ Peacock   Bill Maher   Seamus Dooley

Darren Rooney   Paul Cuddy   Andy Bergin

Declan Conroy   Cyril Cuddy

Eamonn Fennelly   Niall Rigney (Captain)   David Cuddy

Donal Russell   John Shortall   Fionán O'Sullivan

SUBSTITUTES: Nicholas Lacey for Eamonn Fennelly

KILKENNY
BACK ROW L TO R: Henry Shefflin, John Power, Canice Brennan, Andy Comerford, Peter Barry, Eamonn Kennedy, Ken O'Shea
FRONT ROW L TO R: Michael Kavanagh, Tom Hickey, Charlie Carter, Denis Byrne, D.J. Carey, James McGarry, Brian McEvoy, Willie O'Connor

LAOIS
BACK ROW L TO R: David Cuddy, Bill Maher, John Shortall, Eamonn Fennelly, Darren Rooney, Andy Bergin, Declan Conroy, P.J. Peacock
FRONT ROW L TO R: Donal Russell, Fionán O'Sullivan, Niall Rigney, Ricky Cashin, Seamus Dooley, Paul Cuddy, Cyril Cuddy

SUNDAY, 20 JUNE, 1999

LEINSTER SENIOR HURLING CHAMPIONSHIP SEMI-FINAL

OFFALY versus WEXFORD

CROKE PARK

REFEREE: WILLIE BARRETT (TIPPERARY)

RESULT: OFFALY 3-17 WEXFORD 0-15

THE WAY THIS GAME EVOLVED, All-Ireland champions Offaly were never really in serious danger of losing their title. In sharp contrast to the opening game, this semi-final was much more competitive, except that Wexford experienced difficulties in too many positions to mount a more sustained challenge. In the final analysis, Offaly were simply inspired by the scoring of two early goals and by their strength in key areas of the field.

Those early goals, in the 5th and 7th minutes, came courtesy of John Troy and Michael Duignan. They were body blows from which Wexford had to put too much effort into in order to stage a recovery. They did, drawing level ten minutes before half-time, but it left them with little in reserve.

Offaly came into the game with worries about the fitness of three of their players. But, in the circumstances, all three – Kevin Martin, Joe Errity and Michael Duignan – took their places. Their early advantage on the scoreboard reflected their confident play, as well as the experience in the side.

It took Wexford longer than they could have anticipated to settle into the game. The main improvement was achieved in defence – where Liam Dunne was back in the centre after his long lay-off - , and in midfield where Adrian Fenlon was prominent. Up front, team captain Paul Codd was proving the main threat – in general play as well as through his free-taking. Codd was the player who had the teams level in the 25th minute, 2-3 to 0-9. Joe Dooley, excelling in the left corner, hit over a point and then a goal, for Offaly to go in ahead at half-time by 3-6 to 0-10.

Again, for the second half, Wexford were to be outscored. The backs were achieving a degree of consistency in their play, but so were the Offaly players. Hubert Rigney, in particular, was doing great work in limiting Martin Storey. So too was Martin Hanamy. And then there was Brian Whelahan, virtually unbeatable in his traditional right half-back berth. Likewise, Simon Whelahan was very effective in the right corner.

Offaly surged to victory, powered by the excellence of the two Whelahans, Johnny Pilkington, and Paudie Mulhare. Wexford knew that they were beaten by a better team and their defeat marked the end of the road for popular manager Rory Kinsella.

SCORERS: OFFALY – Joe Dooley 1-5; Johnny Dooley 0-6; John Troy 1-2; Michael Duignan 1-0; Billy Dooley 0-2; Ger Oakley 0-1; John Ryan 0-1.
WEXFORD – Paul Codd 0-8; Tom Dempsey 0-2; Ryan Quigley 0-2; Martin Storey 0-1; Rory McCarthy 0-1; Adrian Fenlon 0-1.

OFFALY

Stephen Byrne

| Simon Whelahan | Kevin Kinahan | Martin Hanamy |

| Brian Whelahan (Captain) | Hubert Rigney | Kevin Martin |

Johnny Pilkington   Ger Oakley

| Paudie Mulhare | Joe Errity | Joe Dooley |

| Johnny Dooley | John Troy | Michael Duignan |

SUBSTITUTES: John Ryan for Ger Oakley; Billy Dooley for Joe Errity; Barry Whelahan for Johnny Dooley.

WEXFORD

Damien Fitzhenry

Seán Flood   Ger Cushe   Colm Kehoe

Rod Guiney   Liam Dunne   Larry O'Gorman

Adrian Fenlon   Robert Hassey

Rory McCarthy   Martin Storey   Larry Murphy

Tom Dempsey   Gary Laffan   Paul Codd (Captain)

SUBSTITUTES: Eugene Furlong for Colm Kehoe; Ryan Quigley for Robert Hassey; Michael 'Mitch' Jordan for Larry Murphy

OFFALY
BACK ROW L TO R: Kevin Martin, Michael Duignan, Johnny Pilkington, Kevin Kinahan, Ger Oakley, Hubert Rigney, Joe Errity, Brian Whelahan
FRONT ROW L TO R: John Troy, Simon Whelahan, Stephen Byrne, Martin Hanamy, Joe Dooley, Paudie Mulhare, Johnny Dooley

WEXFORD
BACK ROW L TO R: Larry O'Gorman, Robert Hassey, Adrian Fenlon, Larry Murphy, Gary Laffan, Rod Guiney, Ger Cushe
FRONT ROW L TO R: Liam Dunne, Seán Flood, Martin Storey, Damien Fitzhenry, Paul Codd, Tom Dempsey, Colm Kehoe, Rory McCarthy

SUNDAY, 11 JULY, 1999

LEINSTER SENIOR HURLING CHAMPIONSHIP FINAL

KILKENNY versus OFFALY

CROKE PARK

REFEREE: PAT O'CONNOR (LIMERICK)

RESULT: KILKENNY 5-14 OFFALY 1-16

IT WAS ALL ABOUT MOTIVATION and all about skill on the ball and Kilkenny accomplished their mission with ruthless efficiency. For the second year in a row they defeated Offaly in the final – once more pushing them through the 'back door' – and again, there could be no questioning of the merit of their victory. It was a game in which Kilkenny's goal-scoring power proved the single most important factor.

The opening twenty minutes proved to be the most competitive of the entire game, and provided the best entertainment. Kilkenny's forwards regularly swopped positions and the net effect was to enable Charlie Carter and D.J. Carey, along with newcomer Henry Shefflin, to contribute on a fairly continuous basis. So too, did the speedy Brian McEvoy, showing all the flair and skill he displayed against Brian Whelahan in last year's All-Ireland final.

It was noteworthy, too, that Canice Brennan was very effective in his 'new' position at full-back and that newcomer Eamonn Kennedy was quick to settle in at centre-back. Likewise, footballer Paddy Mullally – the player selected to take the place of the injured Peter Barry – was to more than justify his selection.

While Offaly were well in contention, they were not putting the holders under any serious pressure. And, the failure to do that was highlighted when Kilkenny got the first of their goals in the 20th minute. Created by John Power, it was scored with typical precision by D.J.Carey and it gave the team – and new manager Brian Cody - a terrific boost.

More was to follow, in the shape of a Charlie Carter goal eight minutes later and a third, from D.J. Carey, just before the interval. That came when Carey moved into the edge of the square, perfectly judging the flight of a high ball in from the wing and connecting with it at the right time. Viewed on television, it was a classic goal. Offaly found themselves eight points in arrears, 3-7 to 0-8 and struggling, as they went to their dressingroom.

Just as they had done in last year's All-Ireland final, Offaly moved Brian Whelahan forward on the re-start. He lined out at left half-forward, with Michael Duignan taking over his position. Almost before they had time to settle, Offaly conceded a fourth goal when McEvoy sped away before scoring with a powerful shot.

Now backed by the wind, Offaly did manage to lift the siege, through the efforts of players like Simon Whelahan at corner-back, and, at different stages, strong play from each of the half-backs. In addition, Johnny Pilkington was more forceful around midfield.

The net effect was to see them score five points between the 45th and 55th minutes. But, they also conceded two, and much more importantly, they failed to get the ball into the Kilkenny net when they needed it most. When Offaly did eventually get a goal, courtesy of a determined Johnny Pilkington, it was too late to save them. And, by that stage they were down to fourteen men after substitute Daithi Regan had been sent off and Henry Shefflin had joined the list of Kilkenny goal-scorers.

SCORERS -KILKENNY: D.J. Carey 2-3; Henry Shefflin 1-6; Charlie Carter 1-3; Brian McEvoy 1-1; Andy Comerford 0-1.
OFFALY: Johnny Pilkington 1-3; Johnny Dooley 0-5; Brian Whelahan 0-3; John Troy 0-2; Paudie Mulhare 0-2; Michael Duignan 0-1.

KILKENNY

James McGarry

| Tom Hickey | Canice Brennan | Willie O'Connor |
| Michael Kavanagh | Eamonn Kennedy | Paddy Mullally |

Andy Comerford   Denis Byrne (Captain)

| DJ Carey | John Power | Brian McEvoy |
| Ken O'Shea | Henry Shefflin | Charlie Carter |

SUBSTITUTES: Niall Moloney for John Power

OFFALY

Stephen Byrne

| Simon Whelahan | Kevin Kinahan | Martin Hanamy |
| Brian Whelahan (Captain) | Hubert Rigney | Kevin Martin |

Johnny Pilkington   Paudie Mulhare

| Johnny Dooley | John Ryan | Joe Dooley |
| Billy Dooley | John Troy | Michael Duignan |

SUBSTITUTES: Joe Ernity for Billy Dooley; Daithi Regan for Joe Dooley;
Ger Oakley for Joe Ernity

KILKENNY
BACK ROW L TO R: Henry Shefflin, Brian McEvoy, Canice Brennan, Andy Comerford, Eamonn Kennedy, John Power, Ken O'Shea, Paddy Mullally
FRONT ROW L TO R: Tom Hickey, Charlie Carter, James McGarry, Denis Byrne, D.J. Carey. Michael Kavanagh, Willie O'Connor

OFFALY
BACK ROW L TO R: Kevin Martin, Johnny Pilkington, Michael Duignan, Kevin Kinahan, Hubert Rigney, John Ryan, Brian Whelahan
FRONT ROW L TO R: Billy Dooley, John Troy, Martin Hanamy, Stephen Byrne, Simon Whelahan, Paudie Mulhare, Joe Dooley, Johnny Dooley

SATURDAY, JULY 10, 1999

CONNACHT SENIOR HURLING CHAMPIONSHIP FINAL

GALWAY versus ROSCOMMON

HYDE PARK, ROSCOMMON

REFEREE: JOHNNY McDONNELL (TIPPERARY)

RESULT: GALWAY 4-26 ROSCOMMON 2-8

THIS WAS THE FIFTH SUCCESSIVE STAGING of the revived Connacht hurling final and once again, question marks must be raised about the wisdom of the fixture.

Galway performed much better than in the corresponding game last year, with the new midfield pairing of Clare native Fergus Flynn and the recalled Joe Cooney showing up well.

Galway led by 1-11 to 0-5 at halftime with the goal coming from Kevin Broderick just before the break. Galway went into overdrive in the second half and scored at will. Ollie Canning, Alan Kerins, and the impressive Ollie Fahy all found the net. Colm Kelly, from a penalty and Shane Sweeney had consolation scores for Roscommon.

SCORERS – GALWAY: Ollie Fahy 1-7; Alan Kerins 1-3; Kevin Broderick 1-3; Eugene Cloonan 0-4; Fergus Flynn 0-4; Ollie Canning 1-1; Paul Hardiman 0-1; Joe Cooney 0-1; Joe Rabbitte 0-1; Justin Campbell 0-1.
ROSCOMMON: Colm Kelly 1-1; Brendan Boyle 0-4; Shane Sweeney 1-0; Mickey Cunniffe 0-2; Ray Mulry 0-1.

GALWAY

Damien Howe

Liam Hodgins   Brian Feeney (Captain)   Vinnie Maher

Nigel Shaughnessy   Cathal Moore   Paul Hardiman

Joe Cooney   Fergus Flynn

Ollie Canning   Joe Rabbitte   Alan Kerins

Kevin Broderick   Ollie Fahy   Eugene Cloonan

SUBSTITUTES: Justin Campbell for Eugene Cloonan; Padraig Walsh for Nigel Shaughnessy

---

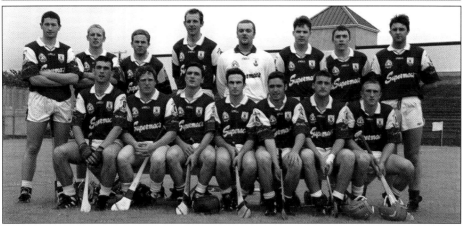

GALWAY
BACK ROW L TO R: Liam Hodgins, Ollie Canning, Kevin Broderick, Joe Rabbitte, Damien Howe, Paul Hardiman, Eugene Cloonan, Brian Feeney
FRONT ROW L TO R: Cathal Moore, Joe Cooney, Ollie Fahy, Nigel Shaughnessy, Alan Kerins, Fergus Flynn, Vinnie Maher

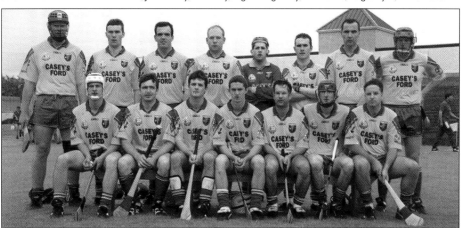

ROSCOMMON
BACK ROW L TO R: Colm Kelly, Brian Mulry, Michael Cunniffe, Paul Connolly, Adrian Tully, Ray Mulry, Enda Gormley, Adrian Kelly
FRONT ROW L TO R: Liam Murray, Damien Lohan, Marty Healy, Pat Finneran. Brendan Boyle, Shane Sweeney, Tommy Healy

SATURDAY, JUNE 19, 1999

ULSTER SENIOR HURLING CHAMPIONSHIP SEMI-FINAL

DERRY versus DOWN

CASEMENT PARK (BELFAST)

REFEREE: PAT AHERNE (CARLOW)

RESULT: DERRY 4-16 DOWN 4-8

DERRY NOT ONLY REPEATED their success of last year over Down, but they did so in dramatic fashion. An eight–point margin testified to the strength of their performance after they trailed by five points with sixteen minutes remaining. Remarkably, Down failed to add to their total after that and were powerless to prevent a Derry take-over, which saw John O'Dwyer hit the last of their goals in the final minute.

Down started the game with a flourish, backed by a strong wind. After a mere five minutes they had a goal and two points on the scoreboard and it was the 9th minute before Derry had their opening score, courtesy of Michael Collins. After that, however, Derry made steady progress to be level by the 21st minute after midfielder Conor Murray scored a goal. And, at the interval, Down enjoyed just a goal advantage, 2-6 to 1-6.

The third quarter was quite competitive with Down again forcing the pace through a Barry Coulter goal immediately after the resumption. And, Paul Coulter scored their fourth in response to their lead being cut to two points.

But, that saw the end of the Down scoring. Two points from Geoffrey McGonigle, another from Ronan McCloskey and then an Oliver Collins goal had Derry in the lead and once there, they built steadily on their advantage. John O'Dwyer's goal ensured their victory before three McGonigle points in injury time produced a marvellous win.

SCORERS– DERRY: Geoffrey McGonigle 0-8; Conor Murray 2-0; Oliver Collins 1-1; John O'Dwyer 1-0 Gregory Biggs 0-2; Michael Collins 0-2; Dermot Doherty 0-1; Ronan McCloskey 0-1; Gary Biggs 0-1.
DOWN – Martin Coulter (Jnr) 1-2; Emmett Trainor 1-2; Barry Coulter 1-0; Paul Coulter 1-0; Jerome McCrickard 0-3; Michael Braniff 0-1.

DERRY

Kieran Stevenson

Emmett McKeever   Davy McCloskey   Damien Kearney

Benny Ward   Declan Cassidy (Captain)   Niall Mullan

Conor Murray   Oliver Collins

Gary Biggs   Gregory Biggs   Ronan McCloskey

Michael Collins   Geoffrey McGonigle   Dermot Doherty

SUBSTITUTES: Barry Kelly for Davy McCloskey; John O'Dwyer for Michael Collins; Michael Conway for Gary Biggs.

DOWN

Graham Clarke

John Brown   Jerome McCrickard   Simon Wilson

Martin Coulter (Snr)   Paul Coulter   Stephen Murray

Gary Savage   John McCarthy

Martin Coulter (Jnr)   Paddy Monan   Barry Coulter

Barry Smith   Michael Braniff   Emmett Trainor

SUBSTITUTE: Paul McCabe for John Brown

DERRY
BACK ROW L TO R: Geoffrey McGonigle, Gary Biggs, Gregory Biggs, Ronan McCloskey, Conor Murray, Dermot Doherty, David McCloskey, Oliver Collins
FRONT ROW L TO R: Michael Collins, Damien Kearney, Declan Cassidy, Kieran Stevenson, Emmett McKeever, Niall Mullan, Benny Ward

DOWN
BACK ROW L TO R: Joe McVeigh (Physiotherapist) Emmett Trainor, Jerome McCrickard, Gary Savage, John McCarthy. Stephen Murray, Graham Clarke, Paddy Monan, Barry Coulter, Frank Dawson (Manager)
FRONT ROW L TO R: Stephen Wilson, Barry Smith, Martin Coulter (Jnr), Martin Coulter (Snr), Michael Braniff, John Brown, Paul Coulter

SATURDAY, JUNE 19, 1999

ULSTER SENIOR HURLING CHAMPIONSHIP SEMI-FINAL

ANTRIM versus LONDON

CASEMENT PARK (BELFAST)

REFEREE: BRENDAN KELLY (WESTMEATH)

RESULT: ANTRIM 3-23 LONDON 1-6

LONDON HURLERS WERE SIMPLY OUT of their depth against the vastly more experienced Antrim side. Antrim wasted no time in establishing their advantage and there was never a stage in the game when they were under serious pressure. Certainly, London gave no hint that they were capable of causing a shock, which they came so close to achieving last year – with the game going to a replay.

Ally Elliott, considered doubtful in advance, was one of the Antrim's stars. Operating at right corner-forward, Elliott contributed two goals and two points before being withdrawn at the three-quarters stage.

Debutante midfielder Conor Cunning teamed up successfully with Johnny Flynn at midfield and a strong half-back line complemented their advantage. Up front, Gregory O'Kane gave good leadership at full-forward.

At the interval, Antrim led by 2-11 to 0-5 and when London lost Timmy Moloney through injury, they struggled in a big way. At the end, London did have the consolation of a late goal, scored by newcomer Fergal Horgan from Seán Treacy's. Antrim were never tested as they might have anticipated and won with twenty-three points to spare.

SCORERS - ANTRIM: Gregory O'Kane 1-9; Ally Elliott 2-2; Gary O'Kane 0-4; Liam Richmond 0-3; John Carson 0-1; Brendan McGarry 0-1; Conor Cunning 0-1; Aidan Delargy 0-1; Padraig McMullan 0-1.
LONDON - Fergal Horgan 1-1; Timmy Moloney 0-3; Mick O'Meara 0-1; Damien Hurley 0-1.

ANTRIM

Shane Elliott

Ciaran McCambridge   Seán Mullan   Ronan Donnelly

Seamus McMullan   Gary O'Kane (Captain)   Padraig McMullan

Conor Cunning   Johnny Flynn

John Carson   Colm McGuckian   Jim Connolly

Ally Elliott   Gregory O'Kane   Liam Richmond

SUBSTITUTES: Brendan McGarry for Jim Connolly; Aidan Delargy for Ally Elliott; Francis McMullan for Johnny Flynn.

ANTRIM
BACK ROW L TO R: Seamus McMullan, Gregory O'Kane, Ronan Donnelly, Ciaran McCambridge, Padraig McMullan, Seán Mullan, Colm McGuckian
FRONT ROW L TO R: Conor Cunning, Liam Richmond, John Carson, Johnny Flynn, Shane Elliott, Gary O'Kane, Jim Connolly, Ally Elliott

SATURDAY, JULY 10, 1999

ULSTER SENIOR HURLING CHAMPIONSHIP FINAL

ANTRIM versus DERRY

CASEMENT PARK (BELFAST)

REFEREE: GERARD DEVLIN (ARMAGH)

RESULT: ANTRIM 2-19 DERRY 1-9

IT REQUIRED A SIGNIFICANT IMPROVEMENT from Antrim in the second half to shake off the determined challenge of Derry. There was every chance of a shock result for almost three-quarters of the game, with Geoffrey McGonigle again inspiring Derry, much as he had done in the semi-final game with Down. But the better balanced Antrim side finished the stronger to advance to the All-Ireland quarter-final.

Antrim dictated the trend of the game from the early minutes, but experienced difficulty in establishing their authority. It was almost a one-man show as Geoffrey McGonigle contributed all of Derry's first-half scores. The half finished with Antrim just two points in front 1-6 to 0-7, thanks mainly to the goal scored in the 24th minute by full-forward Gregory O'Kane.

Derry supporters were given further encouragement when McGonigle ghosted in behind the defence to goal in the 39th minute. Added to an earlier score from McGonigle, it put Derry two points clear.

The lead was short-lived, as Antrim responded positively to the challenge, tightening up in defence and achieving more at midfield. Two points from Liam Richmond had Antrim level before Gregory O'Kane grabbed a point to put them back in the lead.

McGonigle had a chance of a goal from a penalty in the 55th minute, but failed to get in a proper shot and later, a 20-metre free from him was blocked on the line. With that went Derry's slim hopes of victory and when substitute Seán Paul McKillop goaled in the 62nd minute, Antrim were well on course for a comfortable victory.

SCORERS – ANTRIM: Gregory O'Kane 1-5; Ally Elliott 0-4; Seán Paul McKillop 1-0; Liam Richmond 0-3; Francis McMullan 0-2; Gary O'Kane 0-1; Conor Cunning 0-1; John Carson 0-1; Colm McGuckian 0-1; Johnny Flynn 0-1.
DERRY: Geoffrey McGonigle 1-7; Niall Mullan 0-1; Ronan McCloskey 0-1.

ANTRIM

Shane Elliott

Ciaran McCambridge   Owen McCloskey   Seán Mullan

Seamus McMullan   Gary O'Kane (Captain)   Ronan Donnelly

Conor Cunning   Jim Close

John Carson   Colm McGuckian   Brendan McGarry

Ally Elliott   Gregory O'Kane   Liam Richmond

SUBSTITUTES: Seán Paul McKillop for Brendan McGarry; Francis McMullan for John Carson; Johnny Flynn for Ally Elliott

---

DERRY

Kieran Stevenson

Emmett McKeever   Colm McGurk   Niall Mullan

Benny Ward   Declan Cassidy (Captain)   Barry Kelly

Ronan McCloskey   Michael Conway

Paddy McEldowney   Gregory Biggs   Conor Murray

Michael Collins   Geoffrey McGonigle   Dermot Doherty

SUBSTITUTES: John O'Dwyer for Dermot Doherty; Damien Kearney for Benny Ward; Shane McCartney for Geoffrey McGonigle

ANTRIM
BACK ROW L TO R: John Carson, Seamus McMullan, Seán Mullan, Brendan McGarry, Ciaran McCambridge, Colm McGuckian, Jim Close, Ronan Donnelly
FRONT ROW L TO R: Ally Elliott, Gregory O'Kane, Liam Richmond, Shane Elliott, Gary O'Kane, Conor Cunning, Owen McCloskey

DERRY
BACK ROW L TO R: Geoffrey McGonigle, Michael Conway, Michael Collins, Gregory Biggs, Declan Cassidy, Conor Murray, Dermot Doherty, Kieran Stevenson
FRONT ROW L TO R: Benny Ward, Niall Mullan, Barry Kelly, Emmett McKeever, Ronan McCloskey, Paddy McEldowney, Colm McGurk

SUNDAY, JULY 25, 1999

ALL-IRELAND SENIOR HURLING CHAMPIONSHIP QUARTER-FINAL

CLARE versus GALWAY

CROKE PARK

REFEREE: PADRAIG HORAN (OFFALY)

RESULT: CLARE 3-15, GALWAY 2-18 (A DRAW)

THIS GAME HAD EVERYTHING: DRAMA, EXCITEMENT and even a bit of controversy at the end. Most of all it was memorable for the quite remarkable recovery staged by Clare when they stared defeat in the face, nine points down at the three-quarters stage of a marvellous contest. But, displaying the character for which they are renowned, they came storming back, inspired by three goals in a seven minute period. And, in the end, Seán McMahon saved them with two late points from frees.

There had been doubts about the fitness of Ollie Baker, who had been forced off in the Munster final with an ankle injury, but he took his place. Later, eleven minutes into the second half, Jamesie O'Connor made a surprise appearance. The word in advance was that he would not be fit in time, after the hand injury, which caused him to miss the game against Cork.

Galway showed from the very start that they were really fired up for the game. They opened up a three-point lead and would have had a goal but for a typical Davy Fitzgerald save from Ollie Canning.

Brian Feeney had the misfortune to be taken off injured as early as the 8th minute, but his replacement at full-back Michael Healy was to do well. The fact that Clare were making little or no headway in attack, undoubtedly helped.
Vinnie Maher, Paul Hardiman and the inspirational Cathal Moore were all playing starring roles, while Joe Cooney more than justified his selection at midfield. Full-forward Ollie Fahy was to score two goals against Brian Lohan and the first of these, in the 28th minute, was a great boost for their confidence.

Little was going right for Clare, who had brought on P.J. O'Connell and were to introduce Stephen McNamara for the second half. However, two vital scores from Ollie Baker and Seán McMahon kept them in contention approaching half-time when Galway turned over leading by 1-9 to 0-8.

In spite of losing Michael Healy – when he, too, was injured – Galway maintained their grip on the game, eventually stretching their lead to nine points when Fahy scored his second goal.

However, before Galway had time to appreciate their advantage, Clare struck with a goal from Stephen McNamara. Clare's comeback was finally on the way and spectators at home and in the stadium were in for a hurling treat.

Jamesie O'Connor had been 'sprung' from the bench and, despite his lack of match practice, he was to make an important contribution. Nevertheless, what sustained Clare's strengthening challenge were dynamic goals from Niall Gilligan and Alan Markham.

Almost unbelievably, Galway's advantage had been wiped out. Now, it was a case of survival, with the defence quite vulnerable and the forwards being squeezed out as a result of the improvement in Clare's defensive play. In the circumstances, it wasn't surprising to see Clare surge in front, through an Ollie Baker point before Galway showed commendable character.

Ollie Canning equalised before Alan Kerins and substitute Rory Gantley, from a free, put the Westerners two points clear. The margin was back down to the minimum after Seán McMahon pointed a free in the 66th minute and then came the most decisive moment of the game.

Ollie Canning went flying through, after receiving a pass from Joe Rabbitte before letting fly with a powerful shot. It had goal written all over it, except that the ball came back into play off the crossbar. Clare didn't need a second chance and McMahon levelled the scores with a free two minutes from full-time.

Galway might very well have won the match in injury time if they had been awarded – what they maintained afterwards – was a 'definite' free when Ollie Canning appeared to be obstructed.

SCORERS: CLARE – Seán McMahon 0-7; Alan Markham 1-3; Niall Gilligan 1-1; Stephen McNamara 1-0; Colin Lynch 0-2; Ollie Baker 0-2.
GALWAY – Ollie Fahy 2-2; Alan Kerins 0-5; Rory Gantley 0-4; Joe Rabbitte 0-2; Fergus Flynn 0-2; Eugene Cloonan 0-2; Ollie Canning 0-1.

CLARE

Davy Fitzgerald

Brian Quinn   Brian Lohan   Frank Lohan

Liam Doyle   Seán McMahon   Anthony Daly (Captain)

Ollie Baker   Colin Lynch

Fergal Hegarty   Enda Flannery   Alan Markham

David Forde   Conor Clancy   Niall Gilligan

SUBSTITUTES: P.J. O'Connell for Fergal Hegarty; Stephen McNamara for Enda Flannery; Jamesie O'Connor for David Forde

GALWAY

Damien Howe

Liam Hodgins   Brian Feeney (Captain)   Vinnie Maher

Nigel Shaughnessy   Cathal Moore   Paul Hardiman

Joe Cooney   Fergus Flynn

Ollie Canning   Joe Rabbitte   Alan Kerins

Kevin Broderick   Ollie Fahy   Eugene Cloonan

SUBSTITUTES: Michael Healy for Brian Feeney; Rory Gantley for Eugene Cloonan; Peter Huban for Michael Healy.

CLARE
BACK ROW L TO R: Colin Lynch, Brian Lohan, Enda Flannery, Conor Clancy, Davy Fitzgerald, Fergal Hegarty, Frank Lohan, Seán McMahon
FRONT ROW L TO R: Liam Doyle, David Forde, Ollie Baker, Anthony Daly, Brian Quinn, Alan Markham, Niall Gilligan

GALWAY
BACK ROW L TO R: Liam Hodgins, Eugene Cloonan, Cathal Moore, Paul Hardiman, Joe Rabbitte, Brian Feeney, Ollie Canning
FRONT ROW L TO R: Joe Cooney, Vinnie Maher, Ollie Fahy, Damien Howe, Nigel Shaughnessy, Alan Kerins, Fergus Flynn, Kevin Broderick

SUNDAY, JULY 25, 1999

ALL-IRELAND SENIOR HURLING CHAMPIONSHIP QUARTER-FINAL

OFFALY versus ANTRIM

CROKE PARK

REFEREE: MICHAEL WADDING (WATERFORD)

RESULT: OFFALY 4-22, ANTRIM 0-12

ANTRIM NEEDED TO MAKE A GOOD START and to achieve a reasonable level of consistency in order to put up a good showing. Instead, Offaly scored two early goals and it was too easy for them for the remainder of the game.

Nevertheless, it was a victory that was achieved at a cost, with Hubert Rigney first being stretchered off with a leg injury while Kevin Martin followed him with a finger injury, ironically after he had moved into the centre to take over Rigney's position.

Antrim had the benefit of a lead point from Gregory O'Kane inside the first minute, but it was to be the only time in the game that they were in front. Rigney, as usual a very steadying influence at the heart of the Offaly defence, quickly levelled and then Offaly produced a goal virtually out of nothing. The ball came in from a Johnny Pilkington sideline cut and John Ryan finished to the net.

Pilkington himself added a second goal, in the 19th minute, to put Offaly six points clear. Everything was going right for them, with John Troy's clever and skilful play making him a constant threat in attack.

Rigney departed the scene ten minutes before the break, to be replaced by Barry Whelahan and with half-time arriving the game was over as a contest when Offaly had forged an eleven point advantage, 3-8 to 0-6. John Troy scored Offaly's third goal with a delightful effort in the 31st minute.

Johnny Dooley emerged as Offaly's outstanding performer, relishing in his new role as a midfielder. And brother Billy – brought in for John Ryan shortly before half-time – produced a fourth goal fifteen minutes from the end. The final whistle couldn't come soon enough for Antrim.

SCORERS - OFFALY: Johnny Pilkington 1-4; John Troy 1-2; Billy Dooley 1-2; Johnny Dooley 0-4; Brian Whelahan 0-3; John Ryan 1-0; Paudie Mulhare 0-2; Gary Hanniffy 0-2; Hubert Rigney 0-1; Michael Duignan 0-1; Joe Errity 0-1.
ANTRIM: Conor Cunning 0-3; Gregory O'Kane 0-3; Seamus McMullan 0-2; Gary O'Kane 0-1; Colm McGuckian 0-1; Jim Close 0-1; Brendan McGarry 0-1.

OFFALY

Stephen Byrne

| Simon Whelahan | Kevin Kinahan | Martin Hanamy |

| Brian Whelahan (Captain) | Hubert Rigney | Kevin Martin |

Johnny Pilkington   Johnny Dooley

| Paudie Mulhare | John Troy | Michael Duignan |

| John Ryan | Joe Errity | Gary Hanniffy |

SUBSTITUTES: Joe Errity for Billy Dooley; Daithi Regan for Joe Dooley; Ger Oakley for Joe Errity

ANTRIM

Shane Elliott

| Ciaran McCambridge | Owen McCloskey | Seán Mullan |

| Seamus McMullan | Gary O'Kane (Captain) | Ronan Donnelly |

Conor Cunning   Colm McGuckian

| Liam Richmond | Gregory O'Kane | Jim Close |

| Seán Paul McKillop | Ally Elliott | John Carson |

SUBSTITUTE: Brendan McGarry for Seán Paul McKillop

OFFALY
BACK ROW L TO R: Kevin Martin, Johnny Pilkington, Michael Duignan, Kevin Kinahan, Hubert Rigney, Joe Errity, John Ryan, Brian Whelahan
FRONT ROW L TO R: Gary Hanniffy, John Troy, Simon Whelahan, Stephen Byrne, Martin Hanamy, Paudie Mulhare, Johnny Dooley

ANTRIM
BACK ROW L TO R: Seamus McMullan, John Carson, Seán Mullan, Ciarán McCambridge, Ronan Donnelly,
Colm McGuckian, Jim Close, Seán Paul McKillop
FRONT ROW L TO R: Conor Cunning, Gregory O'Kane, Ally Elliott, Gary O'Kane, Shane Elliott, Liam Richmond,
Owen McCloskey

MONDAY, AUGUST 2, 1999

ALL-IRELAND HURLING CHAMPIONSHIP QUARTER-FINAL (REPLAY)

CLARE versus GALWAY

CROKE PARK

REFEREE: PADRAIG HORAN (OFFALY)

RESULT: CLARE 3-18, GALWAY 2-14

THE LESSON HAD BEEN LEARNED by Tipperary earlier in the campaign. Waterford, too, gained an appreciation of it in 1998. You have one chance of beating the Clare hurlers in the championship and Galway realised that before the end of this replay. The principal difference was that Clare's forwards – and Niall Gilligan in particular – sparkled this time. Galway's attack was much more subdued and it was to cost them dearly. For the members of the Clare team there was the sweet satisfaction of rediscovering their best form.

Galway had Eugene Cloonan back in attack, after he was forced off injured in the first half of the drawn match. They also started with Brian Feeney at full-back, but, it was clear from an early stage that he was not fully recovered from the leg injury which limited his appearance the first day to less than ten minutes. Galway also changed their goalkeeper, bringing in Michael Crimmins in place of Damien Howe. While there was little enough between the teams over the opening twenty minutes, Clare looked the sharper. The Banner men led for the first time with an Alan Markham point in the 10th minute and two minutes later came the first of three goals, the scorer being Niall Gilligan.

In the first game, Cathal Moore had been inspirational at centre-back. Now, faced by a highly motivated Conor Clancy, his influence was being curbed to a considerable degree. And, with Gilligan at the top of his form, Clare were not far off their very best.

Galway, nevertheless, remained competitive, thanks mainly to the work of their backs, with Liam Hodgins very effective against Jamesie O'Connor, whose lack of match practice was limiting him. Half-time arrived with Clare leading 1-7 to 0-8, which was not a bad situation at all for Galway, taking everything into consideration.

But, within a minute of the resumption Galway's position worsened when P.J. O'Connell scored a fine goal. Later, as the Clare backs won a stranglehold on the play – Frank Lohan and Anthony Daly, in particular, excelling – Galway's challenge began to weaken. Galway did have the boost of a Eugene Cloonan goal in the 47th minute, which left five points between the sides but after Niall Gilligan got his second goal five minutes later, the game had been decided. It was in injury time when Cloonan got another goal, giving him a highly impressive total of 2-10.

SCORERS: CLARE – Niall Gilligan 2-3; Alan Markham 0-4; P.J. O'Connell 1-0; Seán McMahon 0-3; Colin Lynch 0-2; Jamesie O'Connor 0-2; Stephen McNamara 0-1; Conor Clancy 0-1; Barry Murphy 0-1; David Forde 0-1.
GALWAY – Eugene Cloonan 2-10; Joe Cooney 0-2; Fergus Flynn 0-1; Rory Gantley 0-1.

CLARE

Davy Fitzgerald

Brian Quinn   Brian Lohan   Frank Lohan

Liam Doyle   Seán McMahon   Anthony Daly (Captain)

Ollie Baker   Colin Lynch

Alan Markham   Conor Clancy   P.J. O'Connell

Stephen McNamara   Niall Gilligan   Jamesie O'Connor

SUBSTITUTES: David Forde for P.J. O'Connell; Barry Murphy for Jamesie O'Connor;
Fergie Tuohy for Stephen McNamara.

GALWAY

Michael Crimmins

Liam Hodgins   Brian Feeney   Vinnie Maher

Nigel Shaughnessy   Cathal Moore   Paul Hardiman

Joe Cooney   Fergus Flynn

Alan Kerins   Joe Rabbitte   Ollie Canning

Kevin Broderick   Ollie Fahy   Eugene Cloonan

SUBSTITUTES: Justin Campbell for Kevin Broderick; Padraig Kelly for Brian Feeney;
Rory Gantley for Alan Kerins.

CLARE
BACK ROW L TO R: Colin Lynch, Brian Lohan, Conor Clancy, Davy Fitzgerald, Frank Lohan, Alan Markham,
Seán McMahon
FRONT ROW L TO R: Liam Doyle, Stephen McNamara, P.J. O'Connell, Ollie Baker, Anthony Daly, Jamesie O'Connor,
Brian Quinn, Niall Gilligan

GALWAY
BACK ROW L TO R: Michael Crimmins, Liam Hodgins, Cathal Moore, Eugene Cloonan, Paul Hardiman, Joe Rabbitte, Nigel
Shaughnessy, Brian Feeney
FRONT ROW L TO R: Ollie Canning, Vinnie Maher, Ollie Fahy, Alan Kerins, Fergus Flynn, Kevin Broderick, Joe Cooney

SUNDAY, AUGUST 8, 1999

ALL-IRELAND SENIOR HURLING CHAMPIONSHIP SEMI-FINAL

CORK versus OFFALY

CROKE PARK

REFEREE: DICKIE MURPHY (WEXFORD)

RESULT: CORK 0-19 OFFALY 0-16

THE PITY WAS THAT EITHER TEAM had to lose in this riveting All-Ireland semi-final! Cork and Offaly hurlers produced a classic in a game that represented all the positive aspects of sport. It was a wonderfully exciting and free-flowing game, exactly as one would expect from two very sporting and fiercely determined teams who lit up Croke Park with the quality of their hurling in wet, slippery conditions.

There were emotional scenes at the finish as a young Cork side booked their place in the All-Ireland Final for the first time since losing to Kilkenny in 1992. Brian Corcoran was the only member of the present team that played against Kilkenny seven years ago, and the experienced Erins Own player gave a scintillating display from the centre-half-back position. Corcoran is a player of immense stature and he got it absolutely right afterwards when he said: "It was a brilliant game to win, and terrible to lose".

It was a day Jimmy Barry- Murphy's young charges came of age in a game that produced no fewer than twenty-four scores from play, equally divided between the two teams.

This magnificent Offaly team gave it everything before eventually relinquishing their All-Ireland crown to a late Cork surge, which yielded five unanswered points.

The players made light of the wet and miserable conditions; both defences marked tight, very tight; Brian Whelahan was superb for Offaly while Brian Corcoran was equally impressive for Cork. Johnny Dooley turned in a fine display for Offaly while Mark Landers was very competitive once he settled to the task at hand. No fewer than sixteen players scored – Johnny Dooley, Joe Dooley, John Ryan, Paudie Mulhare, Michael Duignan, John Troy, Johnny Pilkington, Billy Dooley and Brian Whelahan for Offaly with Joe Deane, Fergal McCormack, Seanie McGrath, Mickey O'Connell, Ben O'Connor, Alan Browne and Kevin Murray on the mark for the Munster Champions.

The game began at a frantic pace and it was Offaly who made an early breakthrough with a point apiece from Johnny Dooley, a blockbuster of an effort in the 3rd minute and John Ryan two minutes later. Cork were on level terms by the 8th minute courtesy of a point each from Fergal McCormack and Joe Deane. The Killeagh player had a major impact on the game and emerged as top scorer with ten points. Seanie McGrath scored a wonderful point from play to level the game for the third time, 0-4 each, by the 14th minute. McGrath sped away from Martin Hanamy before sending the ball over the crossbar.

Hanamy, unquestionably one of the most outstanding defenders of his generation, had a difficult afternoon against McGrath firstly and then Ben O'Connor.

Offaly were back in front within seconds when Joe Dooley landed a point. Earlier, Joe Deane scored his second point, only for Michael Duignan to reply almost immediately. Every time Cork scored a point, Offaly hit back with a score of their own for good measure. Deane scored five points for Cork in the closing nineteen minutes while the impressive Johnny Dooley scored three for Offaly with Joe Dooley and the highly-skilful John Troy rowing in a with a point each. Troy showed many of the deft touches and flicks, which marks him out as a hurling artist of rare quality. The manner in which Troy took the ball off Brian Corcoran's hurley early in the second half before firing over a point was simply out of this world! Troy also had a chance of a goal in the 24th minute but the excellent John Browne intercepted and cleared his lines.

Offaly led at half-time by a single point, 0-10 to 0-9, but the scoreline soon changed after the break as Cork hit over four points without reply within five minutes of the re-start. Mickey O'Connell, much more subdued than against Waterford and Clare, started the scoring spree with a splendid point from play and that score was followed by Seanie McGrath, Ben O'Connor and substitute, Alan Browne, who had replaced Neil Ronan before half-time.

John Troy replied with a superb point and further scores for Offaly by Johnny Pilkington and substitute, Billy Dooley, a first-half replacement for Joe Errity levelled the match for the sixth time. Offaly were by now the dominant team and the magnificent Brian Whelahan, Johnny Pilkington and Johnny Dooley fired over a point each to leave the All-Ireland Champions 0-16 to 0-14 ahead. It was a worrying time for Cork, who failed to build on their second half supremacy, and instead allowed Offaly dictate the pace. Indeed, the All-Ireland Champions outscored Cork by 0-6 points to 0-1 between the 43rd and 61st minutes of the second half. Brian Whelahan continued to deliver a tour-de-force display while his younger brother Simon was also outstanding.

But it was then we saw the character of this young Cork side: Kevin Murray reduced the margin to the minimum with a point and then the game took a dramatic turn. John Troy was adjudged to have lifted the ball off the ground and the resultant Cork free was converted by Joe Deane. Exactly 29 minutes and 41seconds had elapsed in the second half when Troy stooped down to get the ball and referee Dickie Murphy immediately blew for a foul. Troy protested but to no avail. Super-fit Cork, inspired by Brian Corcoran and Seán Óg Ó hAilpín, finished strongly with points from Ben O'Connor, Fergal McCormack and Deane. Paudie Mulhare came close to scoring a goal near the end but his shot just skimmed wide of the post and all of Cork breathed a sigh of relief. Those that expressed so little confidence in the side before the Waterford game were now in raptures. Cork have now beaten the 1997 All-Ireland Champions Clare and the '98 Champions Offaly on their way to their first final for seven years.

SCORERS – CORK: Joe Deane 0-10; Fergal McCormack 0-2; Ben O'Connor 0-2;
Seanie McGrath 0-2; Mickey O'Connell 0-1; Alan Browne 0-1; Kevin Murray 0-1
OFFALY: Johnny Dooley 0-5; John Troy 0-2; Johnny Pilkington 0-2; Joe Dooley 0-2; John Ryan 0-1;
Paudie Mulhare 0-1; Michael Duignan 0-1; Billy Dooley 0-1; Brian Whelahan 0-1

CORK

Donal Óg Cusack

Fergal Ryan	Diarmuid O'Sullivan	John Browne
Wayne Sherlock	Brian Corcoran	Seán Óg Ó hAilpín

Mark Landers (Captain)   Mickey O'Connell

Timmy McCarthy	Fergal McCormack	Neil Ronan
Seanie McGrath	Joe Deane	Ben O'Connor

SUBSTITUTES: Alan Browne for Neil Ronan; Kevin Murray for Timmy McCarthy;
Johnny Sheehan for Mickey O'Connell

OFFALY

Stephen Byrne

Simon Whelahan	Kevin Kinahan	Martin Hanamy
Brian Whelahan (Captain)	Hubert Rigney	Kevin Martin

Johnny Dooley   Johnny Pilkington

Paudie Mulhare	John Ryan	Michael Duignan
John Troy	Joe Errity	Joe Dooley

SUBSTITUTES: Billy Dooley for Joe Errity; Gary Hanniffy for John Ryan

---

CORK
BACK ROW L TO R: Diarmuid Ó Sullivan, Brian Corcoran, John Browne, Fergal McCormack, Wayne Sherlock, Donal Óg
Cusack, Seán Óg Ó-hAilpín
FRONT ROW L TO R: Seanie McGrath, Fergal Ryan, Mickey O'Connell, Ben O'Connor, Mark Landers, Neil Ronan, Timmy
McCarthy, Joe Deane

OFFALY
BACK ROW L TO R: Kevin Martin, Johnny Pilkington, Michael Duignan, Kevin Kinihan, Hubert Rigney, John Ryan, Joe Errity, Brian Whelahan
FRONT ROW L TO R: John Troy, Simon Whelahan, Stephen Byrne, Paudie Mulhare, Joe Dooley, Martin Hanamy, Johnny Dooley

SUNDAY, AUGUST 15, 1999

ALL-IRELAND SENIOR HURLING CHAMPIONSHIP SEMI-FINAL

KILKENNY versus CLARE

CROKE PARK

REFEREE; WILLIE BARRETT (TIPPERARY)

RESULT: KILKENNY 2-14 CLARE 1-13

THE GOALS THAT KILKENNY scored at the beginning of the first half and near the end of the second were the scores which saw them through to contest the All-Ireland hurling final for a second successive year. Clare's performance was essentially a mixture of the good and the bad, certainly not up to the standard of their play in the second game with Galway.

Ger Loughnane's team had the misfortune to concede a goal, to Ken O'Shea, after a mere 40 seconds. Discouraging though that might have been, even for a team of Clare's experience, it's value was only to be fully appreciated by half-time. In between, Clare did just about everything except to convert possession into scores. Kilkenny, glad of a reprieve, were to face the second half with great confidence.

Clare had Jamesie O'Connor back in their team and David Forde lined out instead of Stephen McNamara, who had been named at right corner-forward. Niall Gilligan won an amount of good possession at full-forward for Clare.

Pat O'Neill recalled in place of the injured Eamonn Kennedy was very much on top at centre-back for Kilkenny which prompted Clare to move Gilligan on to him later in the half. Clare created the first of four possible goal chances in the 9th minute when David Forde ran through only to see Canice Brennan bodily block his shot. Clare were able to force the pace so well because of the control exerted by their backs. The Banner men were also doing much better at midfield, mainly through the work of Colin Lynch.

P.J. O'Connell was making progress on the left flank, against Michael Kavanagh, but, his influence waned considerably when Peter Barry was moved on to him. In time, the James Stephens man was to play a vital role.

From a position of being vulnerable under pressure, Kilkenny lifted their game to the stage where their own forwards started to threaten. It was to be seen in the promising play of Brian McEvoy. In addition, D.J. Carey was able to make a valuable contribution, while team captain Denis Byrne was to finish strongly at midfield.

Twice in the space of six minutes before half-time Clare lost goal chances. Firstly, goal-keeper James McGarry did well to flick the ball out of Niall Gilligan's reach and then Alan Markham failed from a kicked effort. Shortly after that D.J.Carey had strong claims for a penalty ignored, but, Kilkenny went to their dressingroom at the interval in buoyant mood. They had been outplayed for periods of the half, but they were on level terms, 1-5 to 0-8 – when an improving John Power hit over a marvellous equalising score.

Within fifteen minutes of the second half, Kilkenny had opened up an advantage of four points, two of them coming from Brian McEvoy. Through the combination of speed and good ball control he was to make a vital contribution at left half-forward. Slowly, but surely, Kilkenny began to wear down the Clare challenge, hurling confidently all over the field.

But, their lead was never sufficient to allow them to relax. Clare, showing their renowned battling qualities, refused to wilt and were given a massive boost when Stephen McNamara went through for a goal in the 53rd minute. It was precisely what they needed to strengthen their challenge facing into the most critical phase of the game. However, they reckoned without the genius of D.J.Carey who scored a spectacular goal, less than three minutes later. A high ball came in from a sideline struck from the left flank by Denis Byrne. Carey challenged for it with Henry Shefflin and several Clare backs and he had it in his hands and speeding towards goal before anybody realised it. True to character, his finishing was lethal and Davy Fitzgerald had absolutely no chance of stopping it.

In the remaining time, Clare were reduced to fourteen men after Stephen McNamara was sent off for a second bookable offence and, despite their best efforts, the goal they needed to save the game never looked like coming.

SCORERS – KILKENNY D.J.Carey 1-3; Brian McEvoy 0-4; Ken O'Shea 1-0; Henry Shefflin 0-3; John Power 0-2; Andy Comerford 0-1; Pat O'Neill 0-1.
CLARE – Jamesie O'Connor 0-5; Niall Gilligan 0-3; Stephen McNamara 1-0; David Forde 0-1; Alan Markham 0-1; P.J. O'Connell 0-1; Anthony Daly 0-1; Enda Flannery 0-1.

KILKENNY
BACK ROW L TO R: Philip Larkin, Henry Shefflin, Brian McEvoy, John Power, Canice Brennan, Andy Comerford,
Peter Barry, Pat O'Neill
FRONT ROW L TO R: Ken O'Shea, Charlie Carter, James McGarry, Denis Byrne, D.J. Carey, Michael Kavanagh,
Willie O'Connor

CLARE
BACK ROW L TO R: Colin Lynch, Brian Lohan, Conor Clancy, Frank Lohan, Alan Markham, Seán McMahon
FRONT ROW L TO R: Liam Doyle, David Forde, Ollie Baker, Anthony Daly, Jamsie O'Connor, P.J. O'Connell, Brian Quinn,
Niall Gilligan. MISSING FROM PHOTO: Davy Fitzgerald

Kilkenny's DJ Carey in action against Ollie Baker, Clare,